Poised to PRESENT

Poised to Present (Revised Edition)

A Skills Based Guide for Making Stellar Presentations

Publisher	**Ji-Beom Yoo**
Printed by	**Sungkyunkwan University Press**
Publication date	**February 19 2025**
Writers	**Ray Thomas Hartman**
	Richard John Murray
Project Coordinator	**Yoon You-sook**
Production Editor	**Ku Nam-hee**
Designer	**Kim Saang-bo**

Sungkyunkwan University Press
25-2 Sungkyunkwan-ro, Jongno-gu
Seoul 03063, Korea
Tel 82-2-760-1253~4 **Fax** 82-2-762-7452
http://press.skku.edu
ISBN 979-11-5550-239-6 13740

A Skills Based Guide for
Making Stellar Presentations

Poised to
PRESENT

Sungkyun Language Institute

Sungkyunkwan University Press

CONTENTS

Appendix Section

To the Readers,

Welcome to *Poised to Present*. This text is designed to meet the presentation learning needs of Korean university students. The book covers all vital areas related to presenting, and it is divided according to content and style.

We wrote the book in such a way that teachers can follow it from beginning to end, or they can pick and choose the parts that they consider appropriate for their students. We have also incorporated a range of activities designed to bring the lessons to life and to reinforce what is being taught in the class.

It is important for both teachers and students to reach measurable goals. At the end of the first four chapters you will find a checklist. We included these as a guide for teachers and students. This is in keeping with the mission of the Sungkyun Language Institute, which is to provide the very highest level of goal-oriented learning possible.

We, the writers, hope you enjoy this book and have a positive learning experience.

Ray Thomas Hartman
Richard John Murray

We would like to extend our warm thanks to contributing writer Robert "Bob" Kienzle for his section on *Monroe's Motivated Sequence*.

We would also like to thank Justin Barrass, John Hall, Irene Park, and Malcolm Wray for proofreading and offering constructive criticism on *Poised to Present*.

Finally, we would like to thank Han Jihye, Jang Hye-rim, Jung Sang-bae, and Seo Won for the many long hours they gave up in making the online video presentations.

Ray Thomas Hartman
Richard John Murray

Presentations
Section

What is a presentation?

Any time you speak with someone or to a group, you are, in fact, presenting. For example, every time your professors lecture, they are giving a presentation. A presentation is simply conveying information orally to another person. When we think of presentations, there are two general categories: informal and formal.

An informal presentation is something we do every day. When you meet someone for the first time and introduce yourself, that is an informal presentation. Imagine you are going to meet your boyfriend's or girlfriend's parents; you will think about your appearance, you will consider what you are going to say, and you will focus on what kind of impression you are creating. Also, when you visit your professor's office to talk about something important, that is an informal presentation. For example, you might need to explain why you missed a class, or why you did not do your homework, and yet again, you will present yourself in a certain way. Finally, when you want to recruit new members for your university club, you need to present not only yourself but also your club.

On the other hand, a formal presentation is something we do for important occasions. It might be an academic presentation, a funeral, or a job interview. Whether we like it or not, we will need to make formal presentations at some point in our lives. What are some other situations in which you might be required to present or speak formally to a group?

For the purpose of this course, the emphasis is on how to make the very best formal presentation. We will cover four basic presentation styles, various presentation techniques, and how to get the most out of your presentation tools.

Why do we present?

Simply put, we present because we have something important to say, and we want to communicate it to others.

Before Getting Started

Prior to creating your presentation, it is helpful to think about what you will present and choose an appropriate topic. While you might already know the topic you would like to speak about, sometimes it is necessary to brainstorm ideas and make sure your topic is not too large to discuss in a reasonable amount of time.

Brainstorming: This activity is used to generate ideas related to a particular topic. There are many ways to brainstorm. Let's look at two examples.

Listing: One way to brainstorm is to simply make a list of all the ideas, words, and phrases that come to mind when you think about your topic. The important point here is to get all your thoughts onto paper, no matter how insignificant they may seem. Once you have done this, go back and look at what you wrote. You can then categorize the information into similar groups or use the information to help narrow your topic's focus.

Look at the example below. All of the words and ideas are related to the topic, and now you can either categorize the information into groups like health risks, social aspects, and harmful substances. Also, grouping the information together will help you to focus your topic.

Smoking		
Unhealthy	Nicotine	Smokers/Non-smokers
No smoking areas	Second-hand smoke	Gum disease
Yellow teeth	Tar	Bars/Clubs
Unattractive	Tumors	Age
Cancer	Hard to quit	Bad breath

Now, make a list of all the ideas you think of about one of the following topics.

Globalization / Fashion / Science / Travel / Health / Sports / Business / Culture		

Mind Mapping: Another common technique is mind mapping. Begin by placing your topic in the center of the page and then jot words around the topic, making sure to group similar ideas together and connecting them with lines. When you are finished, your mind map should look like a spiderweb.

Look at the following mind map. Notice how the ideas radiate outward away from the topic. The information moves from general to specific, and the arrows indicate the relationship between ideas.

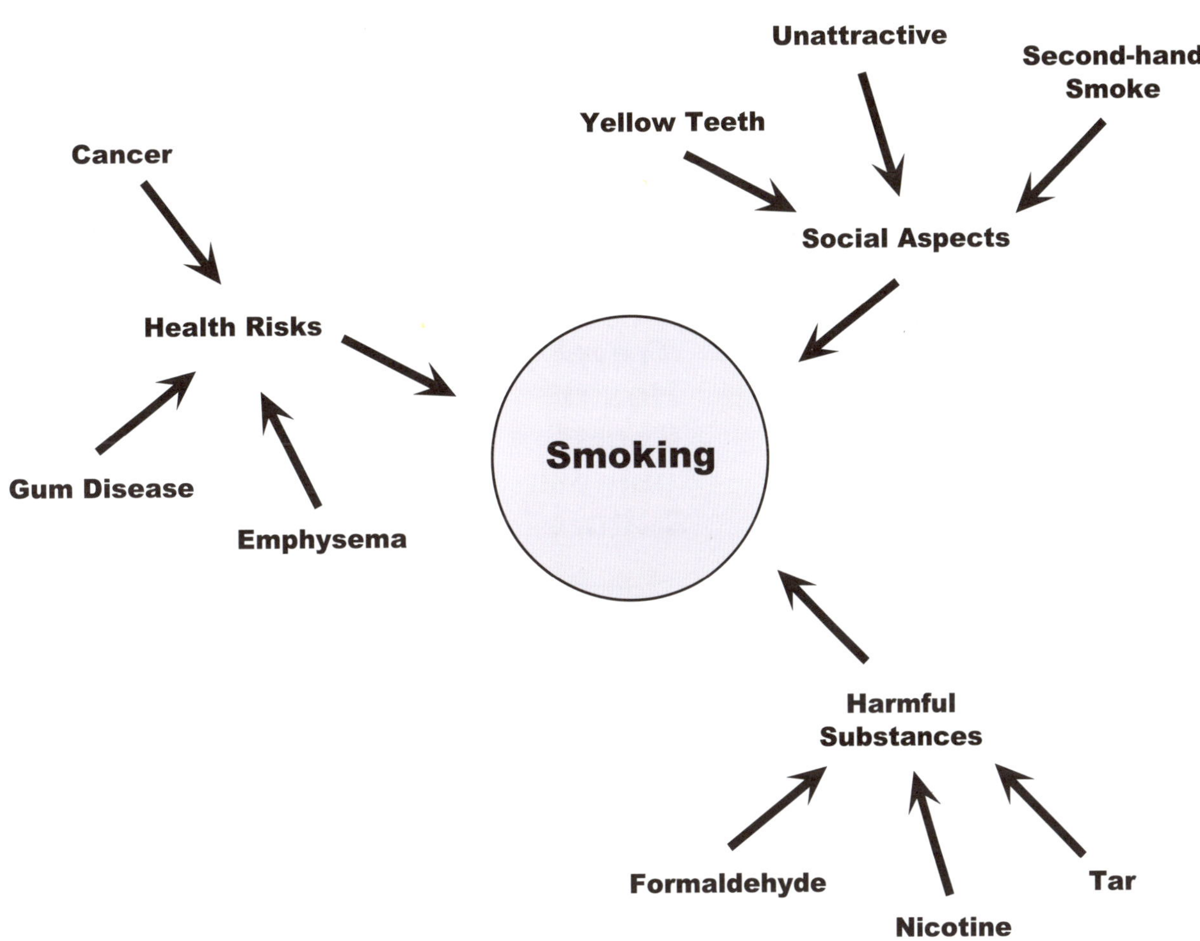

Exercise: Mind Mapping

Now, make a mind map on one of the following topics.

Globalization
Fashion
Science
Travel
Health
Sports
Business
Culture

Narrowing the Topic: If your topic is too wide, you will have a difficult time discussing all of its aspects. Either you will not have enough time because there is too much information to present, or you will omit information. In any case, the overall quality of your talk will suffer.

The purpose of narrowing your topic is to ensure that your topic is focused and not too broad, but be careful, you do not want to narrow your topic too much. If your topic is too narrow, it will be difficult finding enough information to discuss it.

Look at the following diagram. Notice how the information gradually narrows from the large topic "World History" to the more focused and manageable topic "The Sunshine Policy."

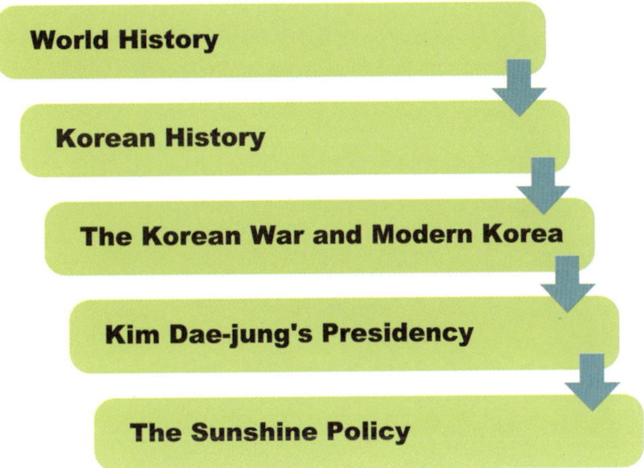

Exercise: Narrow the Topic

Now, narrow these two large, broad topics.

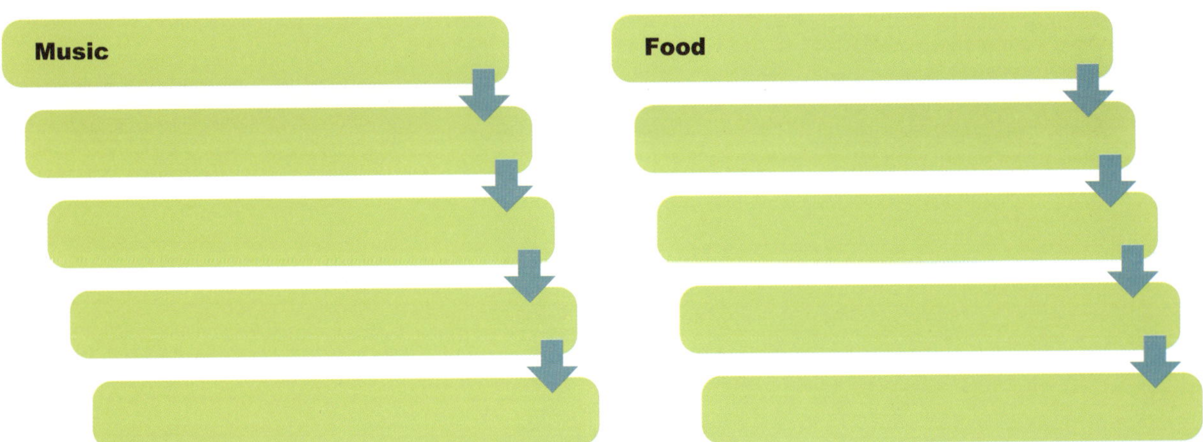

Structure: A General Overview

All presentations contain three parts: an introduction, a body, and a conclusion.

Presentation Structure

I.
The introduction should grab the audience's attention, state the presentation's topic and purpose, and briefly outline the main points to be discussed.

II.
The body should examine each main point in detail by providing support and evidence.

III.
The conclusion should restate the presentation's topic, summarize the main points, and be memorable.

The Introduction

Do you think that first impressions are important? Imagine you are getting ready for a blind date, or you are preparing for a job interview. What kind of first impression do you want to make? Do you want to appear confident and strong or shy and weak? Of course you want to be strong because you know that a strong impression will most likely have a positive influence on the rest of the date or the interview. The introduction is like your presentation's first impression. If it is strong, it will create a solid foundation for the rest of the presentation, and it is not difficult to do as long as you follow these five steps.

Greet the Audience: When you begin your presentation, you must greet your audience. First of all, it is considered polite. Second, it is the first opportunity for you to connect and communicate with the audience, so you are breaking the ice between you and the audience. Finally, by breaking the ice, you will feel more comfortable and relaxed, and the more at ease you are, the better your presentation will be.

Hook the Audience: What is a hook? We use hooks to catch fish, but in presentation's we are not interested in catching fish. We want to catch the audience's attention. Why? Remember, you have something important to say. Otherwise, why would you be giving a presentation? However, you need to encourage the audience to listen to you. You must whet their appetite and appeal to their curiosity. There are several ways to do this.

State Your Topic: Very simply tell the audience what are you going to present about. It is important to tell your audience directly what your topic will be. Avoid being vague and indirect because your audience cannot read your mind. Never assume your audience knows what you will present.

Explain Your Reason: Why are you presenting this topic? What are your goals and objectives? Are you trying to educate the audience? Do you want to persuade them to do something? Is your intention to entertain the audience or to make them think deeply? This is an important question to answer not only for the audience, but also for yourself. Considering your objective will help you find focus and motivation for your presentation.

Give an Overview: What is the first thing you need to do to build a house? Level the ground? No. The first thing is to have a blueprint or a plan. The same is true for your presentation. The overview lets the audience know what you will and will not discuss during your presentation, and it provides an outline for you to follow. Usually, the overview divides the topic into three sub-topics, or main points. Finally, use future tense since these are points you **will** talk about next.

Introduction - Greeting the Audience

This is the first contact you will have with your audience, so it is very important to create a good impression. A good first impression is vital in connecting with your audience and creating relevance, all of which makes you believable as a presenter.

The easiest way to begin is with a basic greeting. This may seem simple, but to greet your audience effectively, you need to know a little about whom they are and how your presentation topic relates to them. This information will help you decide what the most appropriate form of greeting is. Things to consider include cultural, ethnic, age, socio-economic, gender, and religious factors.

For example, if you were making a presentation for a group of middle-aged adults on the future of technology, would you greet them like this?

> "Yo yo yo, watzup my people? My name is DJ Fuzz. I'm an engineering major."

If this were the case, this presentation would probably end as it started: in disaster. Does this form of greeting fit the presenter's audience? No. A better greeting is:

> "Good afternoon ladies and gentlemen. My name is Moon Jeong-eun, and I am a semiconductors and industrial design major."

Greeting the Audience Step by Step

First, greet your audience appropriately.

Jeong-eun has thought about her audience. When she says, "Good afternoon ladies and gentlemen," we can see she has understood that she needs to treat her audience with a degree of respect, and this greeting also sets the tone for a serious presentation.

Second, offer your name.

"My name is Moon Jeong-eun...." Again, this helps build trust and confidence with the audience.

Finally, provide basic credentials.

"I am a semiconductors and industrial design major." Since the speaker majors in these fields, she has expertise in these areas. This shows she is credible.

Exercise: Greeting

Choose three of the following topics, and decide who your audience will be for each topic. Then write greetings for them.

Remember the following structure:

1. Greet the audience
2. Introduce yourself
3. Tell the audience your connection with the topic

- **A brief history of modern Korea**
- **How to become a famous dancer**
- **Why a college degree is necessary**
- **The miracle of Hangul**
- **How to find a boyfriend or girlfriend**
- **My favorite singer**
- **The qualities of an excellent teacher**
- **My dream vacation**
- **What is happiness?**
- **The benefits of regular exercise**

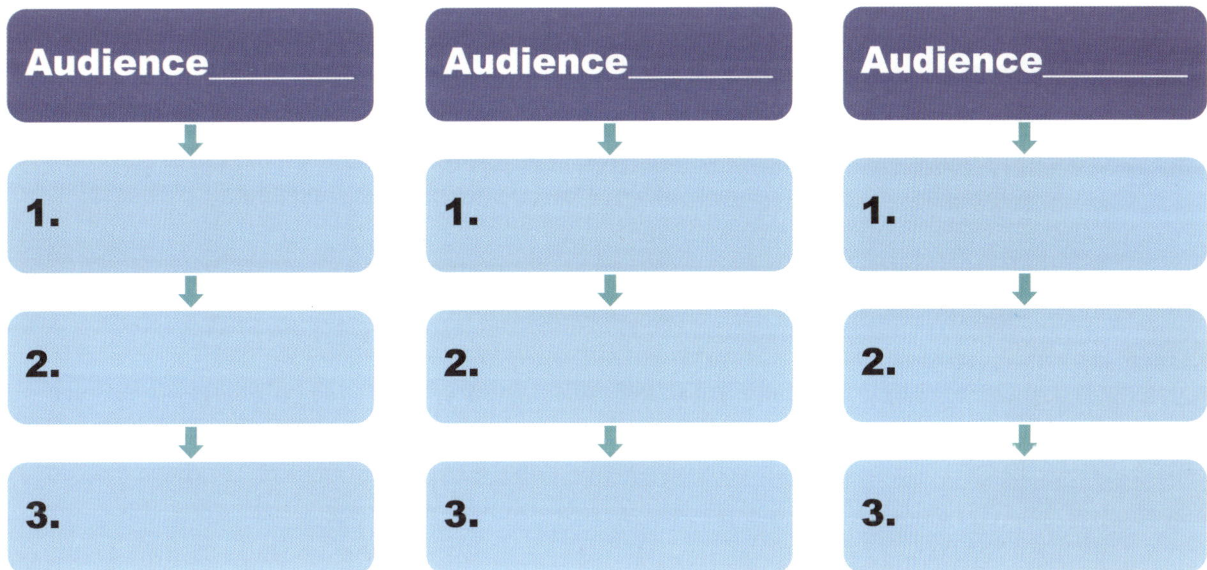

Introduction - Types of Hooks

Popular Misconception

Beginning your presentation by turning what your audience knows on its head is a great way to get their attention. Remember when your parents told you there is no such person as Santa? How did you feel and react? That information certainly got your attention, right?

Interesting or Shocking Fact

Using an interesting fact is a great way to get your audience to say, "Gee, I didn't know that. That's interesting!" When this happens, you have sparked the audience's curiosity, and they will want to know more.

Quote

A quote is what someone has either said or written, and it can make a great hook since people are usually familiar with the quote. This means they have either read or heard it before, and they may understand how it is related to the topic.

Anecdote

An anecdote is a short story which is sometimes humorous, sometimes sad, but always related to the presentation's topic. It is important to keep it brief since a long anecdote will most likely bore your audience.

Rhetorical Question

A rhetorical question is a question that does not need an answer. Why? (That's a rhetorical question.) It does not need an answer because most people already know the answer or know that an answer will be provided by the presenter. What makes this hook work so well is that the answer to the question is usually the presentation's topic or is closely related to the topic.

Example Hooks

Take a look at the following topics and possible hooks you could use.

William Shakespeare	
Popular Misconception	William Shakespeare's birthday is observed on April 23rd, but in reality, his actual birth date remains a mystery.
Interesting or Shocking Fact	Having written 38 plays and 154 sonnets, William Shakespeare's works have been translated into every major language, and his plays have been performed more often than any other playwright's.
Quote	"All the world's a stage, and all the men and women merely players: they have their exits and their entrances; and one man in his time plays many parts, his acts being seven ages." William Shakespeare wrote these poignant words nearly 400 years ago.
Anecdote	Although we do not know which companies William Shakespeare wrote his plays for, by the early 1590s, his plays were performed by his own company, *The Theatre*. What's interesting is that at some point his company had a disagreement with the landlord, so the company leveled *The Theatre* and used its remnants to build the *Globe Theatre*, which is, of course, the most famous theater in the world.
Rhetorical Question	Which English poet and playwright is commonly referred to as the Bard of Avon?

The Korean War	
Popular Misconception	Many people believe that July 27, 1953 marked the end of the Korean War; however, this is not true. North and South Korea are still technically at war with one another; these countries only signed an armistice, not a peace treaty.
Interesting or Shocking Fact	The Korean War is often referred to as the Forgotten War in the US because it was fought between two larger, protracted wars: World War II and the Vietnam War.
Quote	US Army General Douglas MacArthur was quoted as saying to Korean President Sungman Rhee, "I will defend Korea as I would my own country-just as I would California."
Anecdote	On January 12, 1950, just months before the beginning of the Korean War, US Secretary of State Dean Acheson pledged that the United States would fight to defend all territory within its "defensive perimeter," which he defined as including Japan and the Philippines, not Korea. Soviet leader Josef Stalin misinterpreted this statement to mean that he could support North Korean leader Kim Il Sung's "liberation" of South Korea with little risk of intervention by the United States.
Rhetorical Question	Does anyone know the importance of the 38th parallel?

Exercise: Making Hooks

Now, practice making your own hooks with the following topics.

My University Life	
Popular Misconception	
Interesting Fact	
Quote	
Anecdote	
Rhetorical Question	

My Favorite Holiday	
Popular Misconception	
Interesting Fact	
Quote	
Anecdote	
Rhetorical Question	

Introduction - Topics, Reasons, and Overviews

You have introduced yourself and hooked the audience. Now, it is time to state your topic, give reasons why your audience should stay and enjoy your presentation, and offer an overview.

Stating the Topic: Be clear and to the point. Avoid being wordy, and try to limit it to one sentence. The key point is to keep it clear and simple. Do not confuse your audience, and do not make them guess what you will talk about.

Stating the Reason: Make sure to tell your audience why you are giving the presentation. What is the purpose, motive, and style of the presentation, and why should the audience care?
This part should also be clear and to the point.

Stating the Overview: The overview is a map of your presentation. It tells your audience what specific points you are going to make. These are usually divided into three sub-topics, sub-points, controlling ideas, or main ideas.

Example

Imagine your presentation's topic was "How Birds Fly". Below is an example of stating the topic, reason, and overview.

Stating the Topic	"Today I'm going to talk about how birds fly."
Stating the Reason	"Since I was a small child, I have been fascinated by how birds fly, and today I want to shed some light on this phenomenon with you."
Stating the Overview	"My talk will discuss how the physiology of birds allow them to fly. First, I'll look at bone stucture, then muscle development, and finally feathers."

Example Introduction

Good morning, everyone. My name is Kim Jun Hyuk. To get started, I would like to ask you a question. Which is the most heavily militarized border between two countries in the world? You might think it is the border between Israel and the West Bank, but it is not. Actually, it is the Demilitarized Zone between both North and South Korea. Today, I would like to tell you why South Korea is an important focal point in the world. By the end of this presentation, you will have a much better understanding of this vital, yet often overlooked, country. My talk will be divided into three parts: geographical location, economic strengths, and technological advances. Now, let's begin.

Comprehension

Now, answer the following questions.

1. Are all five steps used correctly?
2. What type of hook is used? Is it effective? Why or why not?
3. What is the topic of the presentation?
4. Why is the presenter speaking about this topic?
5. What are the three points the speaker will discuss?

Exercise: Introduction

Now that you have learned about making an introduction, it is time to practice. Make an introduction for the following topics. Remember to include the five steps discussed earlier.

My University Life	
Greeting	
Hook	
Topic	
Reason	
Overview	

My Favorite Holiday	
Greeting	
Hook	
Topic	
Reason	
Overview	

Once you have made the introduction, it is time to move onto the body of the presentation.

The Body

What comes to mind when you think of the word *body*? You might envision a human figure with a head, arms, legs, and a torso, but of all of these things, which one contains the most vital part? You might say the head since it houses our brain, but we can live without a brain (you probably already know someone like this). However, the answer is the torso. This is where most of our vital organs are located, including the most vital of all: the heart.

Just like you, your presentation has a body which contains important information, and this information makes up most of your presentation. In this part of the presentation, you will elaborate on the points mentioned in your introduction's overview.

The Rule of 3

Most people know that a lucky number is seven and an unlucky number is four (unless you are from the West, and then it is "13"), but do you know what the magic number is? It is three. It is also the number of main points given in the introduction's overview. "Why three," you ask. First, consider the following question. How many legs does a tripod need to stand? A tripod only needs to have three legs to stand on its own. One or two legs are not enough, so the tripod will fall down, and four legs are excessive, so the tripod will cost more and be rather bulky and cumbersome. Three is the best option since three is stable and strong.

In addition, three is an important number when it comes to the way our brains work. If someone gives you three pieces of information, the chances of you remembering them is fairly high; however, if that same person gives you four, five, or maybe six pieces of information, what do you think will happen? Most likely, you will begin to forget some of the information you already heard. Thus, if people do not remember most of the important points in your presentation, then you are not communicating well.

Transitions

Let's pretend that you are on the banks of the Amazon River, and you need to cross the river. Unfortunately, you do not have a boat to traverse the river, and swimming across would be extremely dangerous since the river is full of hungry alligators. You desperately need to get to the other side, but in this situation, what should you do? Answer: build a bridge. A bridge is a very useful tool for linking two points together.

Why should you use transitions?

Transitions, also known as signposts, provide signals to the audience. These signals tell the audience when you have finished discussing one point and are ready to move on to the next point. By using transitions, you are helping your audience follow what you say. In fact, you are guiding them point-by-point and step-by-step; thus, your communication is clear, coherent, easy to understand, and easy to follow. Although transitions are small and may seem unimportant, they are vital for making an outstanding presentation. Remember, you have something important to convey, and if your audience cannot follow you, your presentation will be ineffective.

Making a Bridge

Making and using transitions are really easy. Basically, every time you finish one point and are ready to discuss the next one, you need a transition. There are two types: transition words and transition sentences.

Transition Words

First, second, next, and *finally* are examples of transition words. By simply placing these words at the beginning of the sentence, you are making a clear signal to your audience that you are changing points. Be careful! You do not want to use the same transition words again and again. If you do, your presentation will sound dull, boring, and monotonous. Try to incorporate a variety of transition words into your presentation to enhance its overall style, fluency, and effectiveness. Below is a chart of common transition words.

To indicate more information	To indicate an example	To indicate a cause or reason
Also, Besides, Furthermore, In addition, Indeed, In fact, Moreover, Second...Third...,	For example, For instance, In particular, Particularly, Specifically, To demonstrate, To illustrate	As, Because, Because of, Due to, For, For the reason that, Since

To indicate a result or an effect	To indicate purpose or reason	To compare or contrast
Accordingly, Finally, Consequently, Hence, So, Therefore, Thus	For fear that, In the hope that, In order to, So, So that, With this in mind	Although, However, In comparison, In contrast, Likewise, Similarly, Whereas

While transition words are extremely useful when you want to move between supporting ideas within one main point of your presentation, if you use them to transition between main points, things might become a little confusing. Therefore, when transitioning between main points A, B, and C, it is helpful to use transition sentences.

Transition Sentences

If you want to create cohesion and clarity while adding a little style, use transition sentences. As you know, transition words work well between specific supporting ideas, but transition sentences are much better at connecting larger supporting ideas together.

There are two ways to make transition sentences.

Past Time + Future Time
Here, the past time indicates that you have finished discussing the previous point while the future time expresses your intention to move on to the next point.

I **have explained** how Korea's geographical location makes it an important place in the world.

Past Time

Now, I **will discuss** how Korea's economy makes it a vital economic component in today's global business world.

Future Time

Past Time + Rhetorical Question
In this case, the past time states that you have completed one point, and the rhetorical question introduces the next item to be presented.

I **looked at** the large role Korea's economy plays in our ever-growing globalized world.

Past Time

However, **how has** Korea's cutting edge technology made it an important focal point for scientific research and development?

Rhetorical Question

Exercise: Transition Sentences

Below are several main points that need to be connected with a transition sentence. Practice making your own. Remember to use both types. The first one has been done for you.

1. Food in Paris → Sights in Paris

I have explained the foods you can enjoy in Paris. Now, let's look at the sights you can visit.

2. Cleaning your computer → Cleaning the monitor

Past: Future:
Past: Question:

3. Ingredients for kimchi → How to make it

Past: Future:
Past: Question:

4. General Park Jung-hee's character → His domestic policies

Past: Future:
Past: Question:

5. Health benefits of drinking → Social advantages of drinking

Past: Future:
Past: Question:

6. Varieties of wine → Where they are produced

Past: Future:
Past: Question:

7. Types of skin infections → How to prevent them

Past: Future:
Past: Question:

8. Wedding ceremonies → Honeymoons

Past: Future:
Past: Question:

9. Investing in the stock market → Buying gold

Past: Future:
Past: Question:

10. How colds spread → How to protect ourselves

Past: Future:
Past: Question:

What is an outline?

An outline is a system for thinking about, planning, and organizing a presentation.

How to Make an Outline

The directions below not only explain how to make an outline, but they are in outline format as well.

1. State Your Topic:

In one sentence, explain what your topic is.

a. Identify the Main Categories:

What are the primary points you will discuss? These will be the same main points stated in the introduction's overview.

i. Create Sub-Points:

Once you have created the main categories, you need to provide supporting sub-points. This can be any information that supports the main point. For example: data, statistics, facts, examples, and details.

Why should you use an outline?

Do you think top Premier League soccer teams go into soccer matches every week without strategies or plans? Of course not! They do not become some of the best soccer clubs in the world without carefully considering their strategies to win games, and the same is true for you and your presentation. If you want to become a good presenter, then you need to make use of an outline. Outlines are very valuable when creating the body of the presentation since they allow you to see the bigger picture. There are several reasons why you should consider using an outline.

1. When you write an outline, you are generating ideas and transferring them onto paper. In essence, you are performing a type of brainstorming. This is a useful step in the planning stage.
2. As you gather ideas, you will need to organize them. Outlining will help you to decide which organizational pattern is best for your goals and objectives.
3. While you are organizing the information, you will be able to have a clearer idea of what the finished presentation will look like.
4. Finally, you will easily be able to see areas of your presentation that provide sufficient support as well as areas that need more development.

Example Body Outline

Topic: Modern Korea

1. Geographical Location
    a. Center of Northeast Asia
        • Between major world powers
    b. Political importance
        • In regard to North Korea
    c. Military importance
        • US, Japan, ROK Alliance vs North Korea and China

Transition: I have looked at the importance of Korea geographically. Now, let's look at the country's economic strengths.

2. Economic Strengths
    a. Financial and commercial center
        • KOSPI, Korean financial markets
    b. One of the largest economies in the world
        • Comparison of past and present economic indicators (GNP/GDP)
    c. Home to many international corporations
        • Samsung, LG, and Hyundai

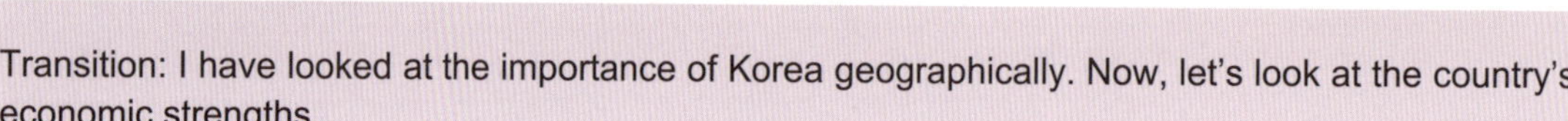

Transition: I have discussed Korea's economic importance in the world, but how do the country's technological advances make it a vital international hub?

3. Technological Advances
    a. Automobile industry
        • Kia, GM Daewoo, and Hyundai
    b. Shipbuilding industry
        • Hyundai Heavy Industries and Samsung Heavy Industries
    c. Semiconductor industry
        • Samsung and Hynix

Exercise: Body Outline

Now, choose one of your topics, either "My University Life" or "My Favorite Holiday", and make an outline for the body of your presentation. Be sure to include three main points and three supports for each main point. Also, practice making transitions.

1. Main Point A: _______________________________

    a. Support 1 _______________________________

       • Examples/Facts/Details _______________________________

    b. Support 2 _______________________________

       • Examples/Facts/Details _______________________________

    c. Support 3 _______________________________

       • Examples/Facts/Details _______________________________

Transition:

2. Main Point B: _______________________________

    a. Support 1 _______________________________

       • Examples/Facts/Details _______________________________

    b. Support 2 _______________________________

       • Examples/Facts/Details _______________________________

    c. Support 3 _______________________________

       • Examples/Facts/Details _______________________________

Transition:

3. Main Point C: _______________________________

    a. Support 1 _______________________________

       • Examples/Facts/Details _______________________________

    b. Support 2 _______________________________

       • Examples/Facts/Details _______________________________

    c. Support 3 _______________________________

       • Examples/Facts/Details _______________________________

You have made it past the presentation body, and now you are in the final stretch, but the presentation is not over yet. You still need to wrap up and conclude your presentation.

The Conclusion

The conclusion is arguably the most important part of the presentation. Unfortunately, many people do not realize this and tend to make mistakes which undermine the effectiveness of their presentation.

Why is the conclusion important?

Think about the last time you watched a movie that had a great storyline, wonderful actors, and believable dialogue. Perhaps everything was terrific except for the end of the movie. The hero and heroine were supposed to fall in love, but they died instead. How did you feel? You most likely felt let down and thought you had wasted your time and money. The same is true for your presentation. The conclusion is the last component of your presentation that your audience will hear. This means what you say in your conclusion will be fresh in the audience's mind. Even if your introduction and body are mind-blowingly fantastic, but your conclusion is weak, then your audience might be left thinking, "That was not a very good presentation." Therefore, how can you make a great presentation? First, let's look at what you should avoid, and next we will look at what you should do.

Mistakes to Avoid

Sometimes presenters feel that the most important part of their presentation is the body because it contains most of the important information they want to discuss. While this is true, it does not mean that you should not work hard to make a strong conclusion. Be careful of these common mistakes.

Avoid Tacking on a Conclusion	There needs to be fluidity throughout your presentation. This is also true for your conclusion. Be sure to transition from the body into the conclusion, making sure your ideas flow smoothly and logically.
Avoid a Mechanical Ending	Do not restate your overview exactly word for word. If you simply copy and paste your overview, it will sound like you did not put any time or effort into planning your conclusion, and you might lose your audience's respect.
Avoid Introducing New Points	This is your conclusion. The purpose is to finish and sum up the main points you have already talked about. The purpose is not to introduce new points. If you have additional points, consider placing them where they belong: in the body.
Avoid Changing Your Stance	Make sure that your opinion and attitude toward your subject do not change at the end. Be consistent and strong, not weak and flimsy.

Parts to Include

Just like the introduction, making a strong, impressive conclusion is not too difficult if you follow these guidelines.

| **Make a Transition** | When you finish the body of your presentation, make sure to maintain your flow by transitioning smoothly into the conclusion. Phrases like "In conclusion", "In summary", or "I have come to the end of my talk" are simple ways to do this. |

| **Restate Your Overview** | Briefly restate the three main points you discussed in your presentation. Make sure to not copy your overview directly from the introduction. Instead, you should say the same things, but you need to use different sentence structures, language, and vocabulary. |

| **Remind the Audience of Important Points** | Certainly, some of the points in the presentation are more important than others. You want the audience to remember these significant pieces of information, so take this opportunity to quickly remind the audience. Remember, the information you provide in the conclusion should leave a lasting impression. |

| **Conclude Memorably** | Do you remember your first kiss? Sure, you do! It was probably a very important milestone in your life, and certainly one that is not easy to forget. Your conclusion needs to be just like your first kiss: memorable. Therefore, how can you make an effective and memorable concluding remark? First, you can use some of the same devices for making hooks. |

| **Wrap Up Well** | Make sure to thank your audience once you have finished. Finally, if there is time, or if the situation presents itself, you may want to invite questions from the audience. |

Concluding Memorably

Below there are some ways to make your presentation conclude well.

Make a Suggestion:
You may want to advise the audience to do or try something, especially if it is something you think is positive.

Give a Warning:
If there is a problem, and we do not solve it, what negative consequences will follow?

Conclude Memorably

Make a Prediction:
What do you think will happen in the future? What do you foresee?

Make a Call to Action:
If you want to motivate the audience to do something or take some action, you should make a strong statement encouraging them to act.

Examples

Take a look at the following topics and possible concluding remarks you could use.

<table>
<tr><th colspan="2" style="text-align:center">William Shakespeare</th></tr>
<tr><td>Suggestion</td><td>The next time you go to the bookstore, why not take a look at the literature written about Shakespeare, and take time to learn more about this fascinating English playwright and poet?</td></tr>
<tr><td>Prediction</td><td>If you have not seen any of Shakespeare's plays performed live yet, then you do not know what you are missing. The next time there is a Shakespearean performance, go and watch it. I guarantee you will be glad you did.</td></tr>
<tr><td>Warning</td><td>Shakespeare's works are classics. Not only will they entertain you, but they will also introduce you to important English literary figures. If you never read them, you will miss out on an extremely important and influential part of English literature.</td></tr>
<tr><td>Call to Action</td><td>Remember, the idea that some other person like Francis Bacon wrote the works attributed to William Shakespeare is preposterous and untrue. We must correct this historical fallacy.</td></tr>
</table>

<table>
<tr><th colspan="2" style="text-align:center">The Korean War</th></tr>
<tr><td>Suggestion</td><td>As you can see, the Korean War was an important turning point in establishing the current global world order. Why not go to your local library and read more on this tragic aspect of Korean history?</td></tr>
<tr><td>Prediction</td><td>If we fail to learn from the Korean War, it will happen again. Maybe not today or tomorrow, but it will happen again.</td></tr>
<tr><td>Warning</td><td>If we do not learn from the errors of our previous leaders, we will be doomed to repeat the same mistakes in the future.</td></tr>
<tr><td>Call to Action</td><td>Do not forget that nearly 40,000 American troops died during the Korean War. It is time to change our attitude toward this conflict; it will no longer be referred to as the "Forgotten War".</td></tr>
</table>

Exercise: Memorable Conclusion

My University Life	
Suggestion	
Prediction	
Warning	
Call to Action	

My Favorite Holiday	
Suggestion	
Prediction	
Warning	
Call to Action	

Example Conclusion

I have reached the end of my presentation regarding South Korea's important role in the world. First, I discussed Korea's geographical importance. Remember that it is located amid many large, industrialized, political, and economic powerhouses. Second, I examined the strength of South Korea's economy. Do not forget that Korea plays a key role in Asian financial markets. Finally, I looked at examples of South Korea's cutting-edge technology. Please keep in mind that this small country is at the forefront of the semiconductor and LCD industries. As you can see, for such a small country, Korea plays a crucial role internationally. Not too long ago, the Korean Peninsula was left devastated by the Korean War. In the relatively short time that has passed, South Korea has transformed itself from a poor third world country to a vibrant star amongst the developed world. This is a feat most countries cannot claim, so the next time someone says, "Korea? Where's that?" Just say, "It's a shining example of Asia." Thank you. Now, if you have any questions, I would like to take time to answer them.

Comprehension

Now, take a minute to answer the following questions.

1. Are all five steps used correctly?
2. Is the presentation summarized using different language, vocabulary, and sentences than in the overview?
3. What are the points the presenter wants the audience to remember?
4. Is the concluding remark memorable? Why or why not?
5. What are some questions you might like to ask the presenter?

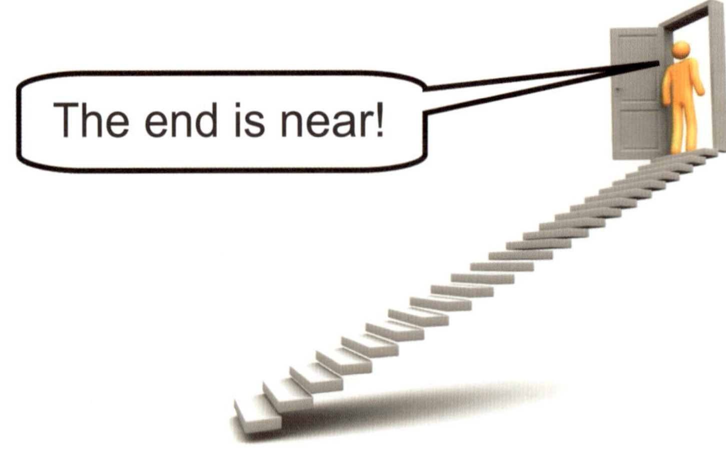

Exercise: Conclusion

Now that you have learned about making a conclusion, it is time to practice. Make a conclusion for the following topics. Remember to include the five steps discussed earlier.

My University Life	
Transition	
Restated Overview	
Points to Remember	
Memorable Concluding Remark	
Wrap Up	

My Favorite Holiday	
Transition	
Restated Overview	
Points to Remember	
Memorable Concluding Remark	
Wrap Up	

Time

When making a presentation, we are usually under some kind of time constraint. It is important to stay within the time specified by your instructor, professor, or boss.

There are many reasons why time is a very important factor. First, time dictates the amount of detail you can go into and the direction of your presentation. In addition, there might be other presenters, and going over time puts undue pressure on them, and it is bad form for you. Finally, your audience will expect you to finish on time, and it is impolite to go over time. Therefore, knowing and sticking to your time limit is vital.

What to Do

After you have planned and written your presentation, it is necessary to practice your presentation. This includes using PowerPoint and any other visual aids while you practice.

Practice your presentation aloud. Having someone listen to you would be ideal, but it is not necessary. Moreover, avoid practicing your presentation in your head because you will probably rehearse your presentation faster than if you say it out loud.

After practicing, if your presentation is too long, you need to take the time to edit it down. You can do this by eliminating unnecessary detail. Conversely, if it is too short, take the opportunity to add more information where it is needed. Then, keep practicing until you fall within the time limitations.

On the day of your presentation, make sure you have any computer files or visual aids that are part of your presentation ready to go. Avoid losing valuable time, and be prepared before your allotted time slot.

Finally, make sure you understand what your time limit includes. If you are required to field questions as part of your presentation, find out if they are included as part of your time limit. Also, know when the clock starts. It might be when you start speaking, or it might be as soon as you reach the front of the room.

Exercise: Keep Your Eye on the Clock

Below there are eight topics. Choose one, and present it to your audience. You have 2 minutes: plus or minus 10 seconds. If you fail to meet the time limit, you must do it again.

Things to do on a rainy day	Life without the Internet
Gift suggestions for your mother or father	Why spending is better than saving
My life in 10 years	How science can solve our problems
Why we should study math	The advantages of being single

Reading

When presenting, it is important to remember that you are **presenting**. You are not **reading**. If you look these two words up in the dictionary, you will quickly discover that they are completely different actions. You must avoid reading your notes to the audience because it is detrimental to your eye contact, body language, voice, and ultimately your connection with your audience. This is discussed in more detail in the Technique section of this book.

Exercise: In Your Words

Work in pairs. Below there are two paragraphs. Read one, and when you are finished, cover it, and summarize it to your partner.

Cities

In the middle of 2007, for the first time in history, more than 50 percent of the world's population was living in cities. This is a trend that is set to continue. In fact, leading urban population experts predict 80 percent of us will be urbanites by 2050. This shift from the countryside to the city has not been without its problems. Overcrowding, pollution, and the massive amounts of resources cities use are issues for all municipal authorities. However, the good news is that cities the world over have been taking steps to make sure their environment is the very best it can be for their inhabitants. In France, Portugal, and Spain, city governments have been creating more "green spaces" by making it mandatory for the owners of tall buildings to plant gardens on their roofs. In Australia and Singapore, city governments offer tax breaks and subsidies to people willing to use low energy techniques and materials in constructing new energy efficient buildings. Not only will this cut down on pollution caused in the generation of electricity, but it will also help to cool cities because buildings will be less reliant on heat-emitting air conditioning units. If more cities take steps to create better environments, the urbanites of tomorrow will rest easy.

Books

The publishing industry has undergone a massive transformation in the last decade because the types of books people buy have changed. Up until a few years ago, the books topping the bestseller lists were fiction. Novels made a huge portion of the average reader's diet. All this has changed. In the past few years, self-help books have been in the ascendency. Books on how to get rich, how to lose weight, how to gain muscle, how to find God, and how to program computers are just a few that have dominated the bestseller lists. This change begs the question: why? The simple answer is, fewer and fewer people are reading for pleasure these days. All too often, we have less free time because we lead more hectic lives, and what spare time we have is divided across more competing activities: cable television and the Internet being the key culprits. Another, and more disturbing reason for our change in reading habits, is that some of us have become more desperate. Instead of taking the time to kick back and relax with a piece of fiction, we are now more inclined to spend that time trying to acquire the answers to some of life's more pressing questions. In others words, we are now reading to get ahead, rather than reading to relax.

Checklist

Introduction	
Greeting	Y/N
Hook	Y/N
Topic	Y/N
Reason	Y/N
Overview	Y/N

Body		
Main Point A	Y/N	
Support 1	Y/N	Transition
Support 2	Y/N	Words
Support 3	Y/N	Y/N
Transition Sentence	Y/N	
Main Point B	Y/N	
Support 1	Y/N	Transition
Support 2	Y/N	Words
Support 3	Y/N	Y/N
Transition Sentence	Y/N	
Main Point C	Y/N	
Support 1	Y/N	Transition
Support 2	Y/N	Words
Support 3	Y/N	Y/N

Conclusion	
Transition	Y/N
Restated Overview	Y/N
Reminders	Y/N
Concluding Remark	Y/N
Thank You	Y/N

Time	
On-time	Great!
15 Seconds Under/Over	Not Bad
30 Seconds Under/Over	Average
45 Seconds Under/Over	Do It Again
60 Seconds Under/Over	Keep Practicing

Effectiveness	
Did Not Read	Spectacular!
Read a Little	Very Good
Read Sometimes	Not Bad
Read a Lot	Try Again
Read All	Keep Working

Rate Yourself	
Excellent	☐
Very Good	☐
Good	☐
Average	☐
Poor	☐

What is an informative presentation?

When you think of the word *inform*, what other words come to mind? Probably *information* or *informant*, but they are all in the same word family with the same root word, *inform*. Instead, can you think of any synonyms that have a similar meaning to *inform*? Now, you might think of words like *notify, advise, enlighten,* and *tell*.

Why do we give informative presentations?

Like the words above suggest, the purpose of an informative presentation is to give the audience information. Your goal and objective is to educate, not to try to convince them to agree with your opinion or to encourage them to do something.

We give informative presentations because we need to communicate information to an audience. For example, a manager might need to advise employees about new company guidelines. A government official may need to notify the public of a policy change. A cancer survivor might want to tell her courageous story. Finally, a preacher may want to enlighten the congregation, so they could lead more virtuous lives. All of these are reasons why people give informative presentations.

Video

Watch the following video of an informative presentation, and answer the questions below.

1. Why is the presenter giving a presentation?
2. What is the topic?
3. What support is given? Is it clear and easy to understand?
4. How is the information organized?
5. Did you learn something new?

Types of Informative Presentations

We will examine three types of informative presentations: demonstrative, descriptive, and definitive.

Demonstrative

This type of informative presentation is discussed in greater detail in another chapter of this book. The purpose of this presentation is to inform the audience of a process or procedure: either how to do or how to make something.

Descriptive

When discussing what something is, we often need to focus on describing its features. For example, what does it look like? Also, we need to examine its characteristics: what is it like? For example, peace is the calm of morning, in which no creatures are stirring, and all is quiet.

Definitive

Sometimes we might need to explain what a new term means, or we might want to clarify an abstract idea or concept. In these cases, you will want to make use of the definitive presentation type.

Imagine you need to define what *love* is. Your answer will probably be completely different from other peoples' because we all have a different idea or concept to define this word. Therefore, being able to clearly define and explain what a term means, or at least what it means to you, is important.

Methods for Defining Terms

Examples

When defining a term, especially an abstract concept like "peace", you may give examples of what that word means.
▶ For example, "peace" is two siblings sharing their toys.

Common Usage

Some words have more than one meaning, and of all those meanings there is one in which the word is most commonly used. Therefore, we can define a word by explaining its common usage.
▶ For example, when I say a family's harmony is important, by harmony, I mean "peace".

Authority

An authoritative definition is how an expert, a professional, or a reference (i.e. a dictionary or an encyclopedia) would define a term.
▶ For example, according to the *Cambridge Dictionary*, "peace" is freedom from war and violence.

Negation

We can define something by explaining what it is not. If someone tells you what something is not, then you will get a clearer picture of what that thing actually is.
▶ For example, "peace" is not hitting your siblings when they take your toys without asking.

Compare and Contrast

Through examining the similarities and differences between two things we are able to get a better idea of what something is and is not.
▶ For example, not only is "peace" freedom from war and violence, but it is also the lack of being interrupted and annoyed.

Exercise: Define "It"

Choose one of the following abstract nouns in the center, and write definitions for it using the five definition methods.

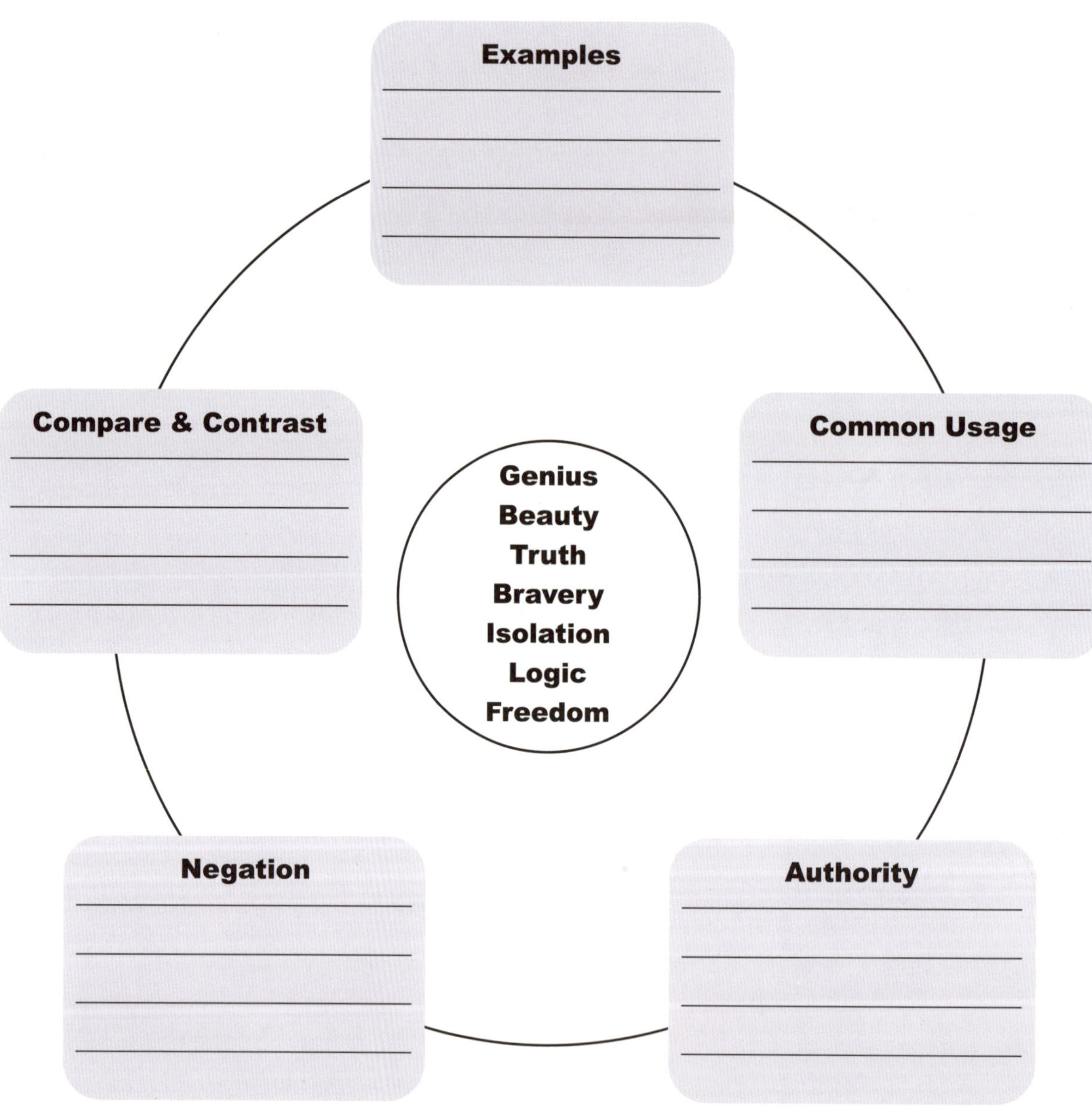

Exercise: Demonstrative, Definitive, or Descriptive?

Look at the following topics, and decide if they are either demonstrative, definitive, or descriptive topics.

1. The functions of a university's student body.

2. Methods for sculpting a statue.

3. The life of Pablo Picasso.

4. Creating your own website.

5. The difference between parachuting and base jumping.

6. The perfect vacation getaway: Las Vegas.

7. Applying for a passport.

8. Five signs that you are in love.

9. Seoul: my home away from home.

10. Preparing the perfect wedding.

11. Explaining the cultural significance of "jung".

12. The different sounds of jazz.

13. Eradicating pests from your home.

14. Meanings of hand gestures in different cultures.

15. Samsung: the driving force of the Korean economy.

16. Maintaining a healthy lifestyle on a vegan diet.

17. Different meanings and characteristics associated with blood types.

18. Changes in men's fashion over the years.

19. The roles of men and women in Korean society.

20. Proper upkeep and care for making your dress shoes last.

Organizational Patterns

Once you have chosen your topic for your informative presentation, you then need to turn your attention to which organizational pattern you should use. Now, do not confuse organizational patterns with structure. The presentation's structure is covered earlier in this book. Structure simply provides a skeleton or framework in which to build your presentation.

Organizational patterns, on the other hand, are guidelines that help you to organize the contents of your presentation's body. There are five organizational patterns you can use depending on your topic and purpose.

I. Topical

This is a very common organizational pattern for informative presentations. When you want to organize your information topically, you should first divide your presentation's topic into three sub-topics. These sub-topics must be closely related to the overall topic yet distinctly different from one another. For example, if you want to present on this topic:

How to lose weight

You might categorize your contents into these three sub-topics:

- ▶ Exercising to lose weight
- ▶ Eating a well-balanced diet to lose weight
- ▶ Calculating and keeping track of your daily calorie intake to monitor weight loss

Exercise: Topical

Look at the following topics. How would you divide them into smaller categories?

1. Preparing for a backpacking trip to Europe
2. Volunteering
3. A memorable childhood experience
4. Choosing a college major
5. Getting a part-time job
6. Your favorite time of the year
7. A person you admire
8. Pollution and the environment
9. Immigrants coming to Korea
10. Guidelines for success

II. Spatial

When you want to describe the features of something, especially what something looks like, then you will use spatial organization. In this pattern, the content is organized according to space and its relation to other things in that space. Imagine you want to describe what your classroom looks like. You might begin your description by panning from left to right, or you might gradually move from the floor to the ceiling, or you might stand in the center of the room and rotate 360 degrees. By organizing your content along these directional movements, you are helping the audience to visualize what you are describing. To help your information flow smoothly, you will need to use special words known as *prepositions*. Prepositions are words that express directional movement and placement. Look at the chart below for some examples.

Next to	In between	From... to...
Under	On top of	Beneath
Along	Following	In front of
Behind	Across from	Inside

Exercise: Spatial Organization

Look at the picture below. Using spatial organization, describe the picture to your partner.

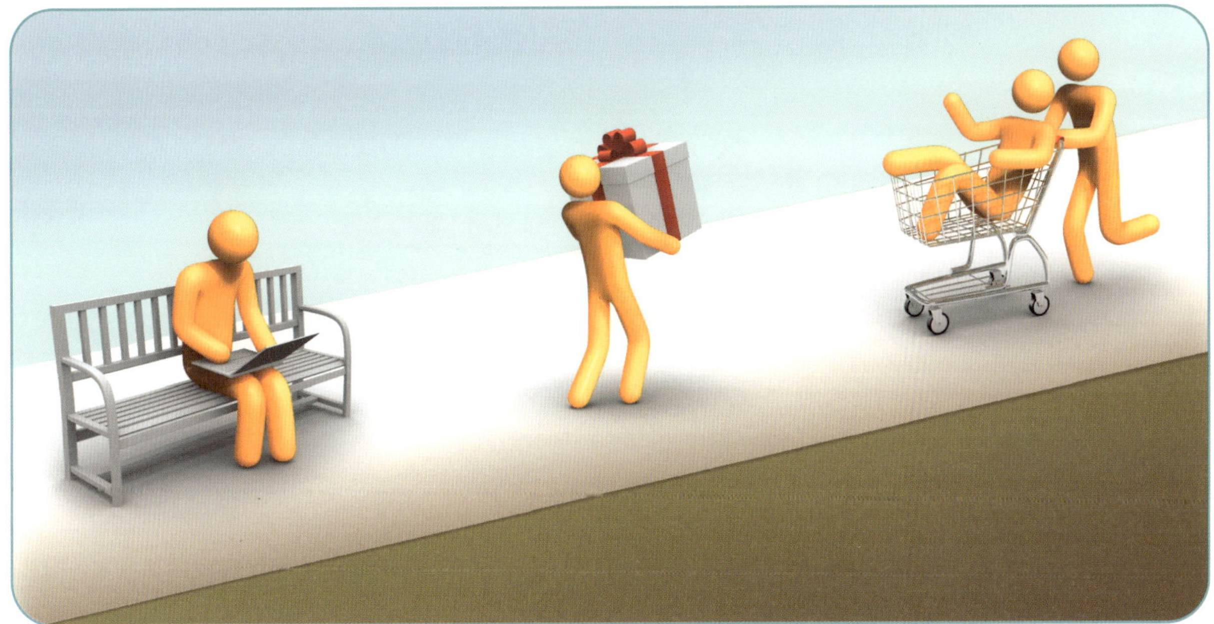

III. Chronological

Chrono is a prefix which means *time*, so contents organized chronologically are explained according to time sequence. This particular pattern is commonly used for demonstrating processes, but could also be used to describe a series of events, for example, the events leading up to the beginning of World War I.

Exercise: Time Sequencing

Choose one historical period, and match the following historical events to their correct years. Put the following historical events into the correct order, and make sure to change the verbs to past tense. Then give an informal presentation to your partner.

Modern Korea

The Gwangju Uprising occurs in May.	1988
On June 25, the Korean War begins.	1979
Seoul hosts the 24th Summer Olympic Games.	1953
World War II ends, and the Korean Peninsula is divided.	1950
The 17th World Cup Games are held in South Korea.	1980
The Korean War is halted with a ceasefire.	2002
President Park Chung Hee is assassinated.	1945

Computer Games

The first home game console, Odyssey, is released.	1982
The popular game *Tetris* is released.	1971
A.S. Douglas creates the first documented computer game. It is tic-tac-toe.	2000
Playstation 2 becomes the first console to use DVD technology.	1952
Mortal Kombat, with its realistic images, becomes an instant hit.	1985
Computer Space becomes the first coin-operated arcade game.	1992
Microsoft enters the PC game market with *Flight Simulator*.	1972

IV. Compare & Contrast

If you are interested in explaining the relationship between two things, you might either want to compare and contrast them with one another to point out similarities and differences. In this pattern, you can either begin by discussing all the similarities, followed by examining all of the differences, or you can examine similarities and differences on a point-by-point basis.

To help you categorize the similarities and differences, you can use a Venn diagram. Below is an example that has already been done for you.

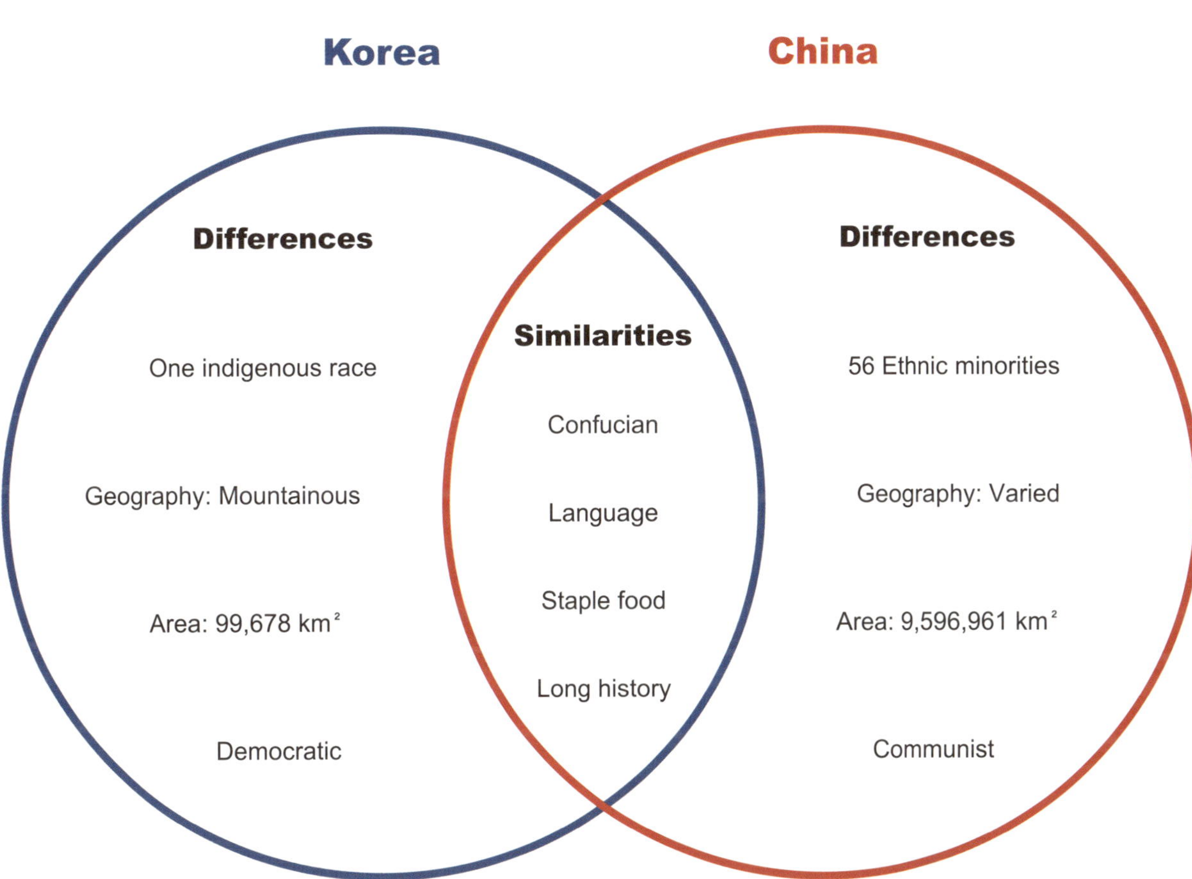

Exercise: Venn Diagram

Make your own Venn diagram comparing and contrasting two things, and prepare to present it in front of your audience.

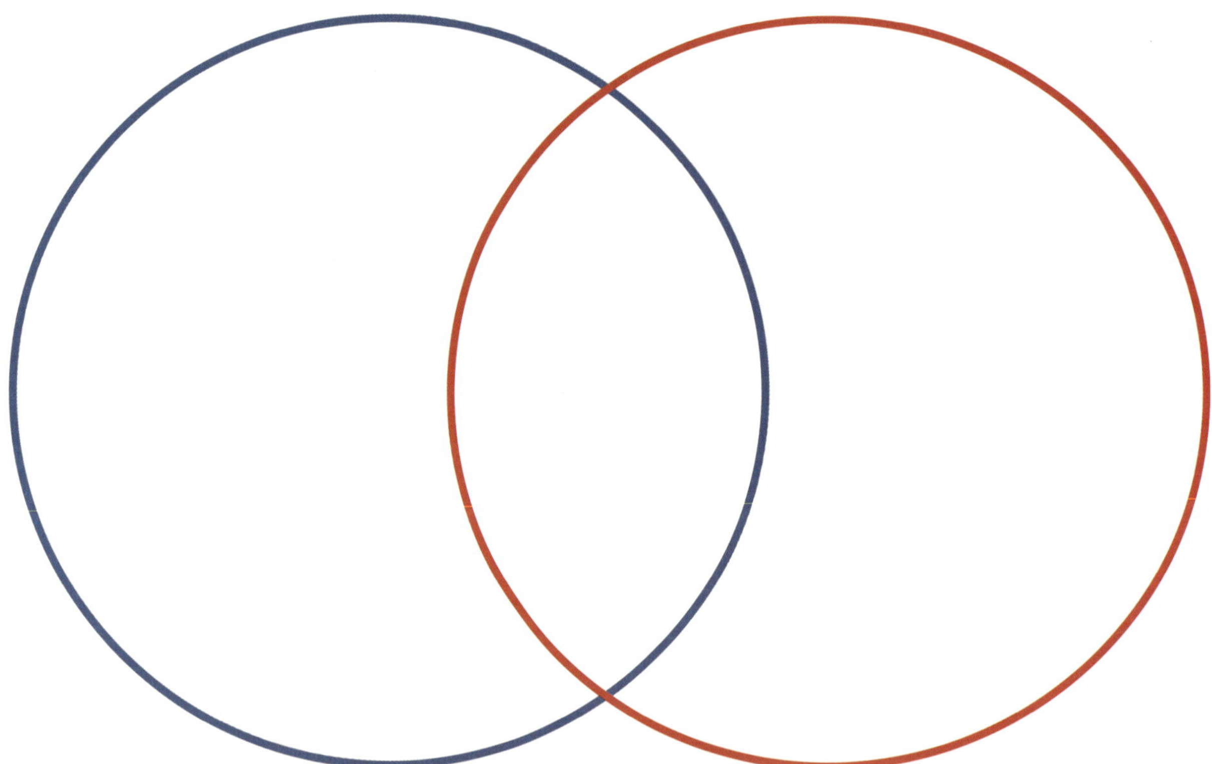

Cause & Effect

We often use this organizational pattern when either explaining a procedure or describing an event and its aftermath. What is nice about this pattern is that you can either begin your presentation by looking at the causes and then discussing the results, or you can present the information the other way around. It is up to you; it depends on your topic, purpose, and objective.

Exercise: Cause & Effect

Look at the following effects. What do think are some causes or reasons for them? Discuss your thoughts with a partner.

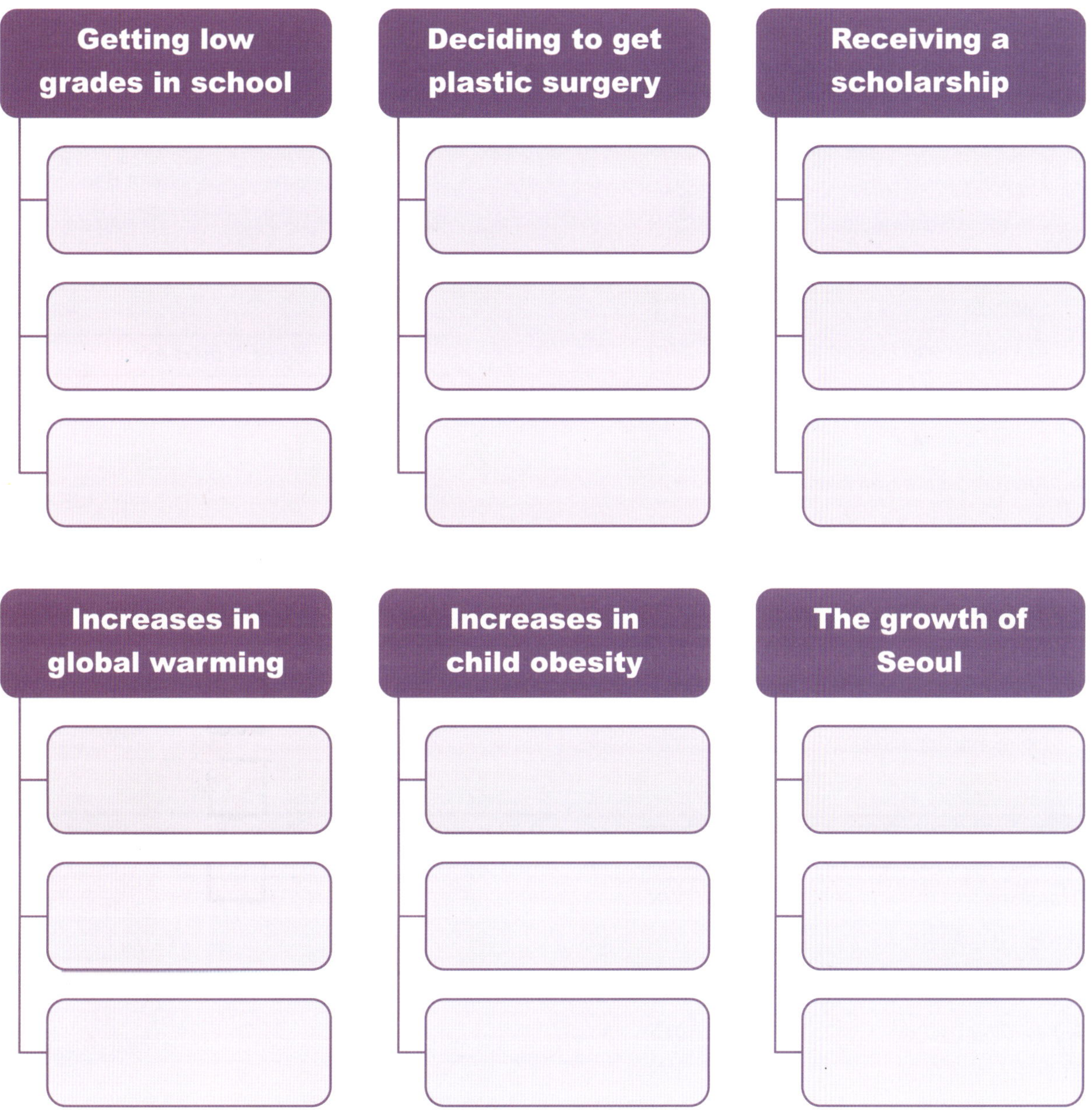

Checklist

Introduction	
Is the purpose clear?	Y/N
What is the purpose?	Y/N
To define a term/concept	☐
To describe something	☐
To demonstrate a process	☐

Body	
Is the content well organized?	Y/N
How is the content organized?	
Topically	☐
Are there 3 sub-topics?	Y/N
Spatially	☐
Are there clear transitions?	Y/N
Chronologically	☐
Are there clear transitions?	Y/N
Comparison & Contrast	☐
Is the content well-balanced?	Y/N
Cause & Effect	☐
Do examples show causality?	Y/N

Conclusion	
Transition	Y/N
Restated Overview	Y/N
Reminders	Y/N
Concluding Remark	Y/N
Thank You	Y/N

Time	
On-time	Great!
15 Seconds Under/Over	Not Bad
30 Seconds Under/Over	Average
45 Seconds Under/Over	Do It Again
60 Seconds Under/Over	Keep Practicing

Effectiveness	
Did Not Read	Spectacular!
Read a Little	Very Good
Read Sometimes	Not Bad
Read a Lot	Try Again
Read All	Keep Working

Rate Yourself	
Excellent	☐
Very Good	☐
Good	☐
Average	☐
Poor	☐

What is a demonstrative presentation?

The purpose of the demonstrative presentation is to explain the steps of an operation, a procedure, or a process. A demonstrative presentation must be dynamic and interesting, meaning you need to actively engage the audience and make sure your topic is meaningful and useful.

This presentation employs a slightly different structure from other presentations. While the introduction and conclusion will remain the same, the body will not follow the *Rule of Three*. Instead of having three main points, the body will be composed of as many steps as the process requires.

Why do we give demonstrative presentations?

If you decide to tell your audience how to prepare *ramen*, make *kimchi*, or get to school, then think again! There is little value in giving information that your audience already knows. Your content must be fresh and offer something of value to your audience. For example, you might discuss how to cook *ramen* without using a stove, how to prepare *kimchi* using foreign ingredients, or how to get to university blindfolded. Always keep in mind, you are offering your audience step-by-step instructions on how to achieve something, how to get something done, or how to get from A to B.

Furthermore, if your presentation is too tedious, the audience will fail to grasp the importance of your demonstration, or they will lose focus during vital steps; thus, wasting not only your time, but the audience's as well.

Video

Watch the following video of a demonstrative presentation, and fill in the blanks of the script on the next page. Also, think about and answer the following questions.

1. What kinds of words were used to fill in the blanks? What is their purpose?
2. What kinds of directions are being given? Why are they being given?
3. How many steps are there to this process?
4. Are the steps clear and easy to understand?
5. Do you think you could follow these directions and make this in your own home?

Sangbae's Special Ramen

I bet you all 5000 won that if I went to your home, I could find one particular item in the kitchen cupboard. Do you know what that item is? Yes, ladies and gentlemen, it is *ramen*. *Ramen* has long been a big part of the Korean diet. It is a quick, low-fuss meal that takes only minutes to prepare. But, what makes *ramen* so special is that we all have our own styles and preferences when it comes to preparing this great dish. My name is Jung Sangbae, and today I'm going to show you how to make "Sangbae's Special Ramen."

__________ you get started with the actual cooking, you need to go to your local supermarket and buy some ingredients. For normal *ramen*, I suggest you go to the noodle aisle and make your selection. My personal favorite is *Shin Ramen* from the good people at the Nong Shim Corporation. For "Sangbae's Special Ramen", you will need *ramen*, eggs, *kimchi*, *mandu* (Korean dumplings), *ddeok* (a type of Korean rice cake), spring onions, onions, and minced garlic.

__________ you arrive home, cut the onions into fine rings, slice the spring onions into two to three centimeter lengths, and fill a pot with about 500 milliliters to a liter of water. __________, put the pot on the stovetop, and __________ the water has started to boil, add the noodles. Allow the noodles to boil for about three minutes.

__________, this is where it gets interesting! Inside the *ramen* packet, you will find the flavoring and seasoning. __________, open the packet, and pour the contents into the boiling water and noodle concoction. __________ you have done this, you have the standard *ramen*. However, for the true noodle connoisseur, this is not enough. I will now put a healthier twist on this very common meal.

The __________ thing you should do is add the onion and garlic to the mix. The onion needs to be added early to make it soft. __________ add the *ddeok* and sliced spring onion. Don't add the *ddeok* too late, or it will be too chewy. __________ a __________ __________, it is time to add the *mandu*. If the *mandu* is frozen, you should add it __________. __________, it is time to add the egg. Break the egg into a small bowl, and beat it with a whisk. __________, pour the egg into the soup.

To __________ __________, get a deep bowl, and pour the *ramen* into the bowl. Mmmmmmm, that smells delicious. All that is left is to eat and enjoy it!

There are many different types of *ramen* on the market and infinite ways of preparing this iconic dish. Today, I have shown you what works for me. The __________ time you have an urge for *ramen*, why not try this style? Your stomach and taste buds will thank you! Bon appétit!

Types of Demonstrative Presentations

There are two general types of demonstrative presentation: directional process and informative process.

Directional process explains how to either make or do something which the audience can replicate. For example, how to bake a cake, how to get to the airport, and how to travel on a budget in India are all directional processes.

Informative process, on the other hand, explains processes that the audience cannot duplicate. For example, how to create world peace, how to improve the prison system, or how to live to be 100 years old are all informative processes.

Exercise: Directional vs Informative

Look at the following topics, and decide if they are either directional or informative processes. Give reasons for your answer.

1. How to become rich in a year.
2. How to win a scholarship.
3. How to become the president of Korea.
4. How to make home brewed beer.
5. How to make salt from salt water.
6. How the Great Pyramids were built.
7. How to remove stains from clothing.
8. How to become a best-selling author.
9. How the United Nations functions.
10. How World War I began.
11. How to write an outstanding essay.
12. How Thomas Edison invented the light bulb.
13. How to remove unwanted hair.
14. How to eradicate illiteracy in third world countries.
15. How the Korean Wave became a trend.
16. How to live a normal life with one kidney.
17. How to apply a tourniquet to a broken arm or leg.
18. How the universe began.
19. How the water cycle operates.
20. How to influence people.

Getting Started:

When preparing for your demonstrative presentation, there are several questions you need to consider.

I. Did I choose a good topic?

When you are brainstorming your topic, think deeply. For example, Laura loves zombie horror movies, and she wants to present *How to Choose a Good Zombie Flick*. While this is not a bad topic, she is worried other students are about to make similar presentations. She wants her presentation to be remembered; she wants an A+. Therefore, she goes back to the drawing board, carefully thinking about her topic and decides on...

HOW TO KILL A ZOMBIE

After taking the time to consider her topic in more depth, she was able to not only wow her audience, but also received the grade she wanted.

II. Did I clearly define special terms and describe the tools I used?

Processes usually involve specialized terms that only experts in the field may understand. These terms are known as *jargon*. Jargon is unnecessarily technical language, and this means it is unnecessarily unclear. Be careful of jargon. Either omit it from your presentation or clearly define the terms during your talk.

III. Did I use logical (chronological) order?

A process is a series of steps that, if followed in the correct order, will result in the creation of something. Therefore, it is necessary that you explain each of the steps in the proper order. Failure to do so will mean that the audience will be misinformed about the procedure, and their efforts to recreate it will be in vain. When going through steps, it is important to use transition words or signposts such as *first*, *second*, *third*, and *last* to indicate the different parts of the process.

IV. Did I explain the steps clearly and accurately?

Not only should you inform the audience of the correct order of the process's steps, but you should make sure to give detailed information about each step, so that it is clear and easy to understand for the reader.

V. Did I use gestures or visual aids?

Although gestures and visual aids are discussed in detail in later chapters, it is important to implement them in your demonstrative presentation. Gestures are natural movements we make with our hands, body, and face to communicate with others. Visual aids consist of anything we can see with our eyes, and these aids help the audience to follow your presentation and understand the process you are describing.

Using gestures and visual aids are very useful and necessary in communicating with your audience. Imagine how difficult it would be to explain how to juggle three balls if you did not use your hands to make the appropriate gestures. In addition, if you want to demonstrate how to build a model train, do you think your presentation would be more or less effective with pictures detailing the step-by-step process?

Exercise: Choosing a Good Topic

Look at the following topics. Which ones do you think are good (/), and which ones are not (X)? Give reasons to support your choices. Finally, how might you change the bad topics to make them better and more interesting? The first one has been done for you.

1. How to make chocolate chip cookies. — Boring.
   - How to make chocolate chip cookies for diabetics. — Better.
2. How to tie your shoe laces.
3. How to survive in the wilderness.
4. How to make the most of your college career.
5. How to start a garden.
6. How to write an essay.
7. How to hold the violin correctly while playing it.
8. How to make ice cream.
9. How to assist the hearing-impaired in class.
10. How to sign up for a class at university.

Exercise: Jargon

Change the boldfaced jargon to a more common and easily understood word. The first one has been done for you.

1. Heeyeon is a *kleptomaniac*.
   - Heeyeon suffers from a disease which causes her to steal things.

2. Ujin's English teacher complained she uses *onomatopoeia* inappropriately in her writing.

3. Soowon has a problem with her *cognitive* ability.

4. I think Chinese food has too much *monosodium glutamate*.

5. Jun-hui took *retrograde anti-virals* in an effort to get over her cold.

6. Jihyeon's dentist told her she needed a filling because she ate too many *complex carbohydrates*.

7. The army was criticized because it inflicted a lot of *collateral damage*.

8. After being attacked by his best friend, Haju had to wear sunglasses because of his *bilateral probital hematoma*.

9. At the gas station, the *fuel transfer technician* filled the car up.

10. The house was uninhabitable after it had been subjected to the effects of *extreme combustion*.

11. When riding her surfboard, Misoo often pulled off *round house cutbacks*.

12. The worst thing about working in an office is being *in the bullpen*.

13. He got fired from the newspaper for not getting the *scoop*.

14. Jeong-eun just bowled a *four bagger*!

15. The countries are working on a number of *confidence building measures (CBMs)*.

Exercise: Chronology

Put the steps into the correct order.

___ Next, clear the ground of any debris, such as leaves or pine needles, and make sure it is level.

___ Finally, fan the fire by blowing air horizontally through the larger branches.

___ Afterwards, place the larger branches over the leaves and twigs, so they form an inverted cone.

___ Once you have these things, find an appropriate place to build your fire.

___ Next, use a match to light the leaves and twigs.

___ Once the larger branches catch fire, you will have a cozy and roaring fire to keep you warm.

___ Next, put the leaves and small twigs in the middle of the circle.

___ Making a good campfire is not as difficult as it seems if you follow these simple steps.

___ First, you will need to gather leaves, small twigs, and large branches.

___ Then place some large rocks on the ground, so they form a circle.

Now, place the following details and explanations with the correct step.

A. Lighting the tinder in several places will help the fire burn more evenly.

B. These rocks will help block the wind and help prevent the fire from spreading.

C. The branches will protect the fire from the wind while allowing the fire to burn efficiently.

D. The oxygen will make the tinder burn hotter and spread more quickly.

E. They will ignite easily and will help the larger branches to catch fire.

F. It is important to find a clear space away from trees to prevent starting a forest fire.

G. Make sure that they are all completely dry. Damp leaves or fresh wood will not burn.

H. This will provide a stable base to build your fire on.

Exercise: Process Ladder (Degrees of Separation)

The ladders below show an object on the top rung and a different object on the bottom rung. Fill in the missing spaces/rungs with the steps needed to move from the top object to the bottom object. The first example has been done for you.

Egg

Crack the egg in a bowl.

Whisk the egg with milk.

Add cheese and ham.

Pour into pre-heated pan.

Cook one side.

Flip and cook the other side.

Omelette

Infant

Senior Citizen

Seed

Seed

Grass

Glass of Milk

Tree

Gum

Telegraph

Cellphone

Wind

Electricity

Cotton

T-shirt

Food

Compost

Avoid These Mistakes

Not Including Your Topic

Be sure to introduce your topic to the audience orally. Avoid launching straight into the steps of your demonstration. Never assume your audience knows what you are going to be talking about even if it is in the title of your presentation.

Not Giving a Reason For Speaking

Not only should you tell your audience what you are going to talk about, but you should tell them why you are talking about this. People want to know why they should listen to a presentation. If you do not tell them why, your audience might not see the relevance of your talk. Remember to emphasize the importance of your talk.

Not Asserting the Nature of the Process

Make sure the audience understands what type of process you are demonstrating. Is it directional, and can they expect to reproduce what you are offering them, or is it informative, and do they understand the limitations they will encounter following your instructions?

Not Offering Detail

A demonstration is more than a list of steps. Vary the transitions you use. For example, do not only use numerical transitions (*first, second, third*). Also, if you do not offer detailed explanations of the steps and how to perform them correctly, then you run the risk of being boring, lacking relevance, and looking foolish.

Not Concluding Strongly

Usually, when people finish explaining the last step of a process, they feel they have concluded their presentation. Although the explanation of the process has ended, the presentation has not. Do not conclude too quickly. As with all presentations, remember to restate your topic, highlight important steps, and give a memorable concluding remark if you want to finish in style.

Checklist

Introduction	
Is the purpose clear?	Y/N
Is the topic meaningful and valuable?	Y/N
What is the nature of the process?	
Directional	☐
Informative	☐

Body	
Are the steps chronologically organized?	Y/N
Are the transitions clear and logical?	Y/N
Are the steps explained clearly in detail?	Y/N
Are needed tools/equipment described?	Y/N
Are special terms defined?	Y/N
Was any jargon omitted?	Y/N

Conclusion	
Are important steps highlighted again?	Y/N
Does the presentation end strongly?	Y/N
Is the process's significance explained?	Y/N

Time	
On-time	Great!
15 Seconds Under/Over	Not Bad
30 Seconds Under/Over	Average
45 Seconds Under/Over	Do It Again
60 Seconds Under/Over	Keep Practicing

Effectiveness	
Did Not Read	Spectacular!
Read a Little	Very Good
Read Sometimes	Not Bad
Read a Lot	Try Again
Read All	Keep Working

Rate Yourself	
Excellent	☐
Very Good	☐
Good	☐
Average	☐
Poor	☐

What is a persuasive academic presentation?

To be persuasive you need to convince the audience that your idea is better than the alternative. To be academic, you should present a balanced and intelligent argument that demonstrates you have a complete understanding of what you are presenting. By combining these two factors, you have the basis for a persuasive academic presentation.

Why do we give persuasive academic presentations?

The answer is in the title. We make this style of presentation to persuade in an informed, academic way. The key to making this kind of presentation is offering relevant evidence that furthers and supports your argument. It is also vital to discredit opposing opinions and create balance. By doing this, you will demonstrate to the audience you are an informed expert on what you are presenting.

Since this is a persuasive academic presentation, you must support your opinion with expert opinions; therefore, you should not use first person. For example, avoid saying, "I think that the death penalty is bad because it impinges on people's right to a good life." Saying "I think", "In my opinion", or "I feel that", shows that you have an opinion. Unfortunately, in an academic sense, your opinion does not count; it is the opinions of experts which matter the most. This will be discussed in more detail in the next part of this chapter.

Video

Watch the following video of an informative presentation, and answer the questions below.

1. What is the presenter's topic?
2. What is the presenter's opinion? Do you agree or disagree? Why?
3. What reasons and support does the presenter give? Are they logical and convincing?
4. If you disagree with the presenter, did the presentation change your mind? Why? Why not?

Using Sources and Evidence

At the heart of an academic presentation are sources and evidence.

Remember, when it comes to academic presentations, your professor is not interested in your opinion alone but is interested in whether or not you can support your opinion with the ideas and opinions of experts on your topic. If you can do this, you will be successful.

Then, how do we define sources and evidence?

Sources

A source is where information comes from. A source can be a book or a newspaper, a website or a journal, a television show or a reliable blog. A source can also be a person. If you quote an authority or expert on your topic, that person is a source. You, too, can be a source. If you go out and conduct your own research, you can also become a primary source.

A secondary source is information that someone else has gathered. It is the information we find in print, online, and on the television or the radio. A secondary source can also be oral information that comments on a primary source.

Exercise: Types of Sources

Categorize the following as either (P) primary or (S) secondary sources.

1. _____ A newspaper article about global warming

2. _____ An interview you conducted with a prominent activist

3. _____ A survey you conducted on preferred restaurants

4. _____ An article you found on the Internet

5. _____ A quote from a famous researcher you found in *The New York Times*

6. _____ A friend you met on the subway

7. _____ Information your professor gave you in class that she got at a conference

8. _____ Something your parents saw in a newspaper

9. _____ A flyer a woman gave you about her sister's restaurant

10. _____ A radio interview with a leading scientist

11. _____ A documentary you watched on television

12. _____ A passage from a book you found in the library

Evidence

Evidence is the information which sources give us. We use evidence to support an argument, making the argument more believable and more credible. Below there are the steps for introducing a source.

First, if the source is a person, we usually start by introducing the person's title. Titles like Mr., Mrs., Miss, or Ms. tell us whether a source is male or female, married or unmarried. More importantly, titles such as Prof., Dr., or Rev. can indicate whether or not your source is academically, professionally, or spiritually credible. Titles can also denote rank within an organization. Examples of this include what we find in the military or the police, such as PFC, Sgt., Col. and Gen.

As a general rule, we only use a title if the title is of notable importance, for example Dr., Prof., or Col. These days, it is not always politically correct to denote a person on the basis of gender or marital status, so do not do it. Note: if you are unsure about whether to use Miss, Mrs., or Ms., choose Ms. as it is the least offensive to some women.

Secondly, give the source's name. This step is straight-forward and easy; however, try to keep the style of the names consistent. For example, if you start quoting Kim Minji, do not later refer to her as Minji Kim. This will only confuse your audience.

Finally, tell the audience why this person is a valuable source. To do this, you need to give the source's position. For example, if you are making a presentation about the death penalty, your source should be an authority on the subject.

This is incorrect:

"According to my friend Nami, the death penalty is good for the following reasons..."

Who is Nami? Why should we care what Nami has to say on the subject? Is Nami an authority on the subject? We do not know.

This is correct:

"According to Prof. Park Nami, <u>the Chairperson of the Korean Parliamentary Sub-Committee for the Extension of the Death Penalty</u>, the death penalty will serve society in the following ways..."

Now we know who Nami is. We can trust Nami as an authority on the subject. Therefore, by quoting Nami as a source, your argument has more credibility and is more persuasive.

Exercise: Introducing Sources

Introduce the following sources.

1. Your English teacher has asked you to make a persuasive presentation on the issues facing foreigners living in Korea. You have decided to use your teacher as a source. How would you introduce your teacher as a source?

According to ____

____

2. You are going to make a presentation on the importance of joining a university club. Who would you choose as a source and how would you introduce this person?

____

____

3. You have been asked to make a persuasive presentation on the necessity of plastic surgery. Introduce a credible source.

____

____

4. You listened to an interview from leading economist Paul Prenter. How would you use him as a source?

____

____

5. You are making a presentation on the dangers of drinking too much. You go out on a Friday night and meet a very drunk man who tells you about his health problems related to drinking. You decide to use him as a source in your presentation, but you did not get his name. How can you introduce him as a source?

____

____

Using a Source Again

Remember, evidence is the information you take from your sources, and one source can offer more than one piece of evidence. If this is the case, you do not need to continue reintroducing your source. However, you must make reference to that source.

For example:

"According to Prof. Park Nami, the Chairperson of the Korean Parliamentary Sub-committee for the Extension of the Death Penalty, the death penalty will serve society in a number of ways. **Prof. Park** said the death penalty is the best way for the families of victims to get closure after the death of a loved one. **She also** said the death penalty acts as a deterrent for those toying with the idea of committing a capital crime."

Rather than saying, "Professor Park Nami, the Chairperson of the Korean Parliamentary Subcommittee for the Extension of the Death Penalty", every time you want to use this source, you can simply refer to her as "Professor Park" (her title and surname), and later as "she" (the appropriate pronoun).

Exercise: Referring to a Previous Source

The following evidence all comes from the same person, Dr. Lee Junseok. Dr. Lee is a cancer specialist at Johns Hopkins University Hospital in the United States. Your presentation is on the dangers of smoking. On a separate piece of paper, using Dr. Lee's evidence below, introduce the source and offer two additional pieces of evidence.

- ▶ "Smoking as a teenager increases the chances of developing lung cancer later in life by two hundred percent."
- ▶ "People, who have parents who smoke, are more likely to become smokers later in life."
- ▶ "Heavy smoking not only leads to lung cancer, but it can also lead to tongue and throat cancer, heart disease, and it can have a detrimental effect on the people around the smoker."
- ▶ "It is a common misconception that smoking helps reduce stress. If anything, long term smoking puts more stress on our bodies, and that can lead to deterioration in both physical and mental health."
- ▶ "The cost of smoking to society is incalculable. Every year, hospital beds that could be taken by more deserving patients are occupied by people suffering from smoking related diseases."

Non-human Sources

The style we use for non-human sources is similar to human sources. Make sure you include the name of your source and why the source is relevant to your argument.

For example, if you decide you want to quote from a newspaper you would say:

"According to an article from the January 22nd edition of the *Joong-ang Ilbo*, Korea's leading daily newspaper, 52 percent of adult Koreans support the use of the death penalty."

Never assume your audience will understand the significance of your source. You might think all Koreans know about the *Joong-ang Ilbo*. This is probably true, but what if you have a foreigner in the audience?

Remember to be specific with your sources. Avoid the following:

"According to *Naver*, a famous website..." This is like saying, "According to someone, a person..."

Counterarguments

When making an academic presentation, it is vital to recognize both sides of the argument. If you only present one side of an argument, you are stating an opinion. This is not academic.

To be academic you need to present a counterargument. The counterargument is the opposing argument to the one you are presenting.

Why Use Counterarguments?

Including a counterargument demonstrates you understand the issue you are dealing with in full. It creates objectivity and balance, and if employed properly, it makes your argument more persuasive. Also, a counterargument outlines the salient points of the opposing argument, and it helps your audience understand the argument completely.

Making a Counterargument

Structuring a counterargument is easy if you follow this simple approach.

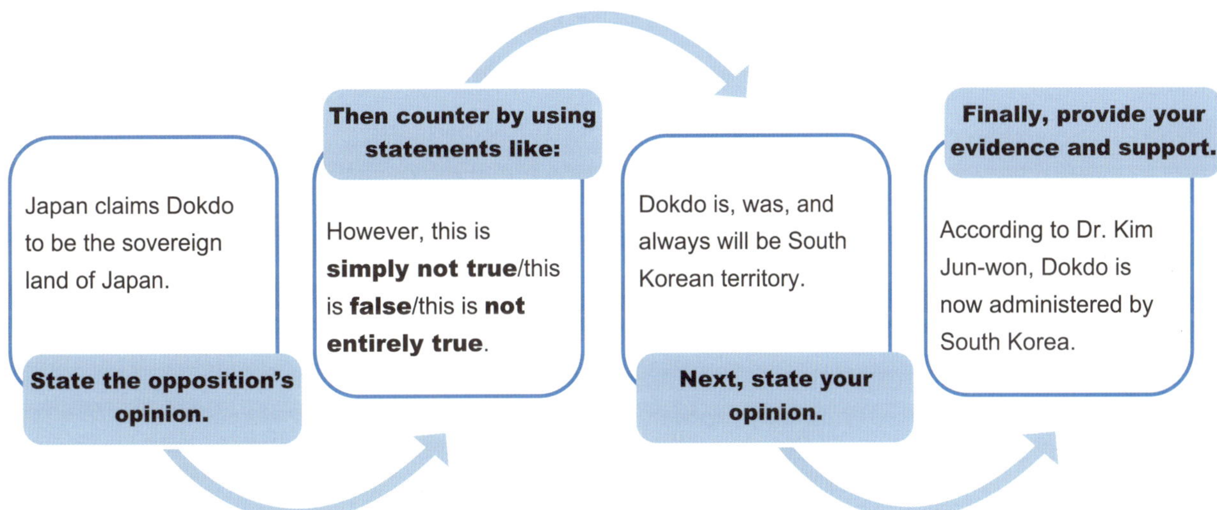

Exercise: Countering

Follow the previous steps, and write counterarguments for the following statements.

1. The death penalty acts as a deterrent for potential criminals.

____

____

2. Plastic surgery gives the recipient confidence.

____

____

3. As citizens, women must also serve in the military for the defense of the nation.

____

____

4. Owning a pet is irresponsible if you live in the city because pets need space.

____

____

5. North Korea should not be given aid if it is only going to be used for the military.

____

____

6. Smokers should be allowed to smoke wherever they want.

____

____

7. Foreigners living in Korea have an obligation to learn the Korean language.

____

____

8. All university students should receive a living allowance from the government.

____

____

9. All freshman students must join a university club.

____

____

10. Income tax should be paid on a voluntary basis.

____

____

Structuring the Counterargument in the Presentation

There are a number of ways to structure your counterargument in your presentation.

The first way to include your counterargument in your presentation is to mention it in the introduction.

Introduction

First, introduce the counterargument along with your opinion. This will give you more time to convince the audience your argument is stronger.

Body 1

Give your first supporting argument and provide evidence such as reliable facts, statistics, data, and expert opinions.

Body 2

Give your second supporting argument and provide evidence such as reliable facts, statistics, data, and expert opinions.

Body 3

Give your third supporting argument and provide evidence such as reliable facts, statistics, data, and expert opinions.

Conclusion

Conclude your presentation. Remind the audience one last time that the opposing opinion is fallible by restating the original counterargument.

Another advantage of this style is that if the argument and the counterargument do not match exactly, you do not need to refute the counterargument on a case by case basis. You are refuting the opposition's argument on a macro-level. Remember, you do not need to say the counterargument is wrong. Your mission is to demonstrate your argument is better and ultimately more persuasive than the alternative.

The second way to present the counterargument is to introduce it point-by-point within each body point. This means that in each body point you start by mentioning the counterargument to the opinion you are about to argue, and then refute that counterargument.

Introduction	Introduce your opinion along with an overview of the main points you will examine. Do not discuss the opposing opinion at this time.
Body 1	Present and support your first argument while countering and refuting your opposition's argument.
Body 2	Present and support your second argument while countering and refuting your opposition's argument.
Body 3	Present and support your third argument while countering and refuting your opposition's argument.
Conclusion	Conclude your presention by reiterating your opinion to the audience as well as restating the reasons you hold that position.

An advantage of this style is you can show a direct compare and contrast relationship between your opinion and the opposition's opinion on a point-by-point basis. It leaves little room for misinterpretation on the part of the audience since you are breaking the argument down on a micro-level.

Countering Continued

Your instructor has asked you to make a persuasive presentation on why the death penalty should be banned. You decide to argue in your first body point that the death penalty does not serve as a deterrent to crime. How would you structure this including a counterargument? Look at the following.

Supporters of the death penalty argue the death penalty acts as a deterrent, meaning criminals are less likely to commit a crime if they face the prospect of being executed if caught and convicted. However, there is ample evidence that points to the contrary. In the American state of Texas, the death penalty has a long history. According to Prof. Michael Bailey, a criminologist with the Texas Department of Corrections, the death penalty had little or no effect on reducing the rate of crimes punishable by death. "When a person kills another person, they never expect to be caught," Prof. Bailey said. "There is no expectation of what the eventual outcome could be," he said. Prof. Bailey also pointed to the fact that when compared to American states that do not have the death penalty, the incidence of capital crimes in Texas per capita is much higher...

You will notice in this example, the counterargument is short. In a 5-10 minute persuasive presentation, you need to give as much time to your argument as possible. Therefore, avoid offering too much information and detail in your counterargument. Keep it brief, and put more weight on your argument.

Exercise: Countering Continued

You are making a presentation on the benefits of dual citizenship. Write a body point giving the counterargument to your opinion, and then, using your imagination, offer sources and evidence to back up your argument.

Logic

When making a logical argument, it is important to avoid the following logical fallacies.

Stereotyping	This logical fallacy assumes groups of people, who share physical, racial, national, or emotional characteristics, are exactly the same. ▶ For example, all Englishmen are gentlemen.
Circular Logic	This logical fallacy states that the cause results in the effect, and the effect creates the cause. ▶ He reads many books to become smart, and since he is smart, he reads many books.
Post Hoc Fallacy	This logical fallacy has a problem with the cause and effect relationship. ▶ For example, there are many tall Koreans who eat kimchi; therefore, eating kimchi makes you tall.
Argument Ad Hominem	This logical fallacy attacks the opponent's character, not the argument itself. ▶ For example, people, who think that Dokdo is Japanese territory, are stupid.
Argument Ad Populum	This logical fallacy relies heavily on emotion, not logic, to make an argument. ▶ For example, if you fail to enter into a top ranked university, you will never succeed in life.
Bandwagon	This logical fallacy dictates that because the argument is popular, you should follow it. This is also know as *peer pressure*. ▶ For example, wearing flip flops in winter has become trendy. Although it is ridiculous, you wear them in order to be accepted.
Nonsequitur	This logical fallacy arises when the conclusion is not a direct result of the evidence. ▶ Cows destroy the ozone layer, so eating beef will protect the environment since there will be fewer cows.

Exercise: Logic

Look at the following statements. Identify what type of logical fallacy it is, and explain your answer.

1. He is from New Zealand. He will know a lot about sheep.

2. All of the people on my street own a red car. Tomorrow I'm buying a red car.

3. Even though I know it is bad to smoke, I'm going to smoke because my friends do.

4. Many pretty girls drink iced coffee, so if you drink iced coffee, you will become beautiful.

5. Burning gas destroys the ozone. Drive your car, so there will be less gas to burn.

6. Most geniuses eat cabbage. Eating cabbage will stimulate your brain to levels of genius.

7. You can't criticize my town. You are not from here.

8. People who don't like cricket are idiots.

9. Tall guys are good at basketball.

10. Eat your dinner. There are starving people in Africa.

11. Two dogs were fighting, so there is a hole in the wall.

12. He is tall because he drinks milk, and the milk he drinks makes him tall.

13. You need to get married before you are 30, or you will never find happiness.

14. He rides a motorcycle and has tattoos, so he must be a bad guy.

15. She smokes cigarettes, so she must be from a bad family.

16. I always fly business class, so I am better than the people in economy.

17. He has really long hair. Are you sure he is not a woman?

18. People who think I'm good looking have great taste.

19. All rich people drive luxury cars.

20. If you don't eat your dinner, you can't have any dessert. How can you have any dessert if you don't eat your dinner?

Checklist

Introduction	
Is the opinion clear?	Y/N
Is the intention clear?	Y/N
• Does it call for change?	☐
• Does it call for action?	☐

Body	
Makes good use of sources for support?	Y/N
Introduces sources clearly?	Y/N
Provides a variety of sources?	Y/N
Sources are relevant?	Y/N
Makes good use of counterarguments?	Y/N
Counterarguments are persuasive?	Y/N

Conclusion	
Provides a clear conclusion?	Y/N
• Offers a solution?	☐
• Makes a call for action?	☐
• Gives a prediction?	☐

Time	
On-time	Great!
15 Seconds Under/Over	Not Bad
30 Seconds Under/Over	Average
45 Seconds Under/Over	Do It Again
60 Seconds Under/Over	Keep Practicing

Effectiveness	
Did Not Read	Spectacular!
Read a Little	Very Good
Read Sometimes	Not Bad
Read a Lot	Try Again
Read All	Keep Working

Rate Yourself	
Excellent	☐
Very Good	☐
Good	☐
Average	☐
Poor	☐

What is a seminar?

Seminars are different from other forms of presentations. A regular presentation is largely oneway communication: the presenter makes a presentation to the audience offering new and/or detailed information on a theme or topic.

A seminar differs because the presenters elicit the response and opinions of their audience in a formalized way. To begin with, a small group of students, five to six, make a group presentation to the class on a topic they have researched. At the conclusion of the presentation, the presenters each take a small number of the audience and teach them about their topic and discuss the issues in more depth.

The presenters usually give their groups a packet of information related to their topic. This might include a newspaper or magazine article, general discussion questions, reading comprehension questions, and vocabulary questions. This package is often given to the audience members the class prior to the seminar which gives the audience time to familiarize themselves with the material.

Why are seminars important?

Seminars give presenters the opportunity not only to present on their chosen topic, but also to teach students about their topic in detail. This gives the students the chance to ask questions, and it gives the presenter an opportunity to teach the subject. Being able to teach a topic demonstrates the presenter has complete knowledge of the topic and takes an interest in it.

Seminars are also important because the audience gets a diverse understanding of the topic. In the presentation, the audience can glean a basic understanding. However, when they read the related article, they can get a better understanding of how the topic relates to contemporary society. Also, through reading, discussing, and completing vocabulary exercises, they can improve those respective skills.

Finally, through the seminar process, the presenters can hone their management, organizational, and interpersonal skills. It truly benefits all those involved.

Example Seminar I

Watch the following group presentation, and then in groups complete the following exercises.

Pre-Reading Questions

1. How would you define *plastic surgery?*
2. Do you know someone who has had plastic surgery?
3. Have you ever considered plastic surgery?
4. Do you know what "Beauty is in the eye of the beholder" means?
5. What do you think "Beauty is only skin deep" means?

Vocabulary

Match the definition to the correct word in the column on the right.

1. (adjective) describes goods, products, and places that are of very high quality	groom
2. (noun) a period of ten years	rafters
3. (verb) to prepare someone for a special job or activity	augmentation
4. (adjective) expensive and only for people who are rich or of a high social class	decade
5. (noun) someone who studies or is an expert in sociology	upscale
6. (noun) a set of actions which is the official or accepted way of doing something	sociologist
7. (noun) any of the large sloping pieces of wood which support a roof	queuing
8. (noun) the act of increasing the size or value of something by adding something to it	exclusive
9. (adjective) existing very commonly or happening often	prevalent
10. (verb) to wait in a line of people, often to buy something	procedure

Paper for Plastic?

Ten years ago, South Korea had the highest savings rates in the OECD. A **decade** on, South Korea has among the lowest savings rates. Walking around the streets of Seoul, it is not hard to see where the money has gone. The roads teem with luxury European cars. Department stores are filled to the **rafters** with the latest French and Italian fashions which young and old alike are **queuing** to buy. However, this consumption goes more than just skin deep.

Sujin Kang describes herself as a normal Korean university student. Like other Korean women of her age, she loves to spend time shopping and dining in, and around, Seoul's **upscale** shopping districts. She loves to spend time with her boyfriend. She goes to church with her family on Sunday, and, like many of her generation, she has had plastic surgery.

I met Sujin at a coffee shop in the **exclusive** Seoul neighborhood of Apgujeong. Over lattes, she explained that plastic surgery was no big deal. She claimed that almost all her friends had had 'something' done.

According to Dr. Shin-woo Park, a plastic surgeon with a practice in Apgujeong, the most common **procedures** are nose jobs, breast **augmentation**, and the double eyelid, a procedure in which the eyelid is cut to create a fold. However, do not think that plastic surgery is only confined to women. "I'm getting more and more male clients," Dr. Park said.

To understand the popularity of plastic surgery in Korea, it is important to understand Korean society. According to American **sociologist** Prof. Frank Choi, Korea is among the most competitive societies in the world.

"From the day a Korean baby enters the world, he or she is **groomed** for success," Prof. Choi said. "Success can be measured by the university people attend or the company they work for." Prof. Choi went on to say parents look for every opportunity to give their children an edge, both academically and physically.

"All job applicants need to submit a recent photo as part of a job application. Applicants are scored on their appearance, so it is little wonder plastic surgery is as **prevalent** as it is," Prof. Choi said.

As Koreans continue to search for an edge over the next person, the trend towards plastic surgery looks unlikely to change in the future.

"If my son or daughter were unhappy with their appearance, I'd have no problems paying for them to get plastic surgery. After all, it's my money, and I'll spend it how I want to," Sujin said.

Comprehension Questions

1. Who is Sujin Kang?
2. According to Dr. Shin-woo Park, what are the most common types of plastic surgery?
3. According to Prof. Frank Choi, how is success measured in Korea?
4. What do job applicants need to submit with their applications? Why?
5. What would Sujin do if her children were unhappy with their appearance?

Discussion Questions

1. Do you think plastic surgery makes a person more confident? Why or why not?
2. What do you think are some of the risks of having plastic surgery?
3. How would you feel if your spouse or significant other had plastic surgery?
4. What is the difference between cosmetic surgery and plastic surgery?
5. Would you ever get plastic surgery? If so, where and why?
6. Is it reasonable to judge job applicants on their physical appearance?
7. Should plastic surgery be covered by health insurance?
8. Should failed plastic surgeries be covered by health insurance?
9. Should children be able to have plastic surgery? Explain.
10. Should plastic surgery be banned or regulated by the government?

Notes

Example Seminar II

Watch the following group presentation, and then in groups complete the following exercises.

Pre-Reading Questions

1. Are you familiar with the term *capital punishment?*
2. What does "An eye for an eye" mean?
3. Have you or someone you know ever been a victim of crime?
4. Do you know some countries that carry out the death penalty?
5. Do you know what Korea's stance on the death penalty is?

Vocabulary

Look at the **boldfaced** words in the article, and match them to their definitions.

1. (verb) to get rid of completely or destroy something
2. (noun) when something is very important and deserves respect
3. (verb) to search a place or container in a violent and careless way
4. (verb) to find a way in which two opposing situations or beliefs can agree and exist together
5. (noun) the official name for the regional grouping of European countries
6. (noun) someone who is too young to have the legal responsibilities of an adult
7. (noun) a growth of strong feeling among a large group of people
8. (noun) the part of you that judges how moral your own actions are and makes you feel guilty about bad things that you have done or things you feel responsible for
9. (verb) to become rough or cause something to become rough
10. (adjective) very unhappy

Now, use the words above to fill in the blanks below to complete the sentences.

A. My ex-girlfriend and I could not ________________ our differences.
B. The farmer spent his day ________________ insects using pesticides.
C. The government did not expect the ________________ of opposition against the new policy.
D. My room was so messy it looked like it had been ________________ by a thief.
E. The holes in his shoes made him feel ________________ in winter.
F. In Korea, ________________ cannot drink or smoke.
G. The government charged her with ________________ because she was a spy.
H. The ________________ of marriage is one of the foundations for a strong family.
I. He felt his hands ________________ because of all the manual labor.
J. Hitler was the first to introduce the idea of the ________________________.

Death Penalty: Hanging in the Balance?

We live in a world dominated by issues. Climate change and global warming, war in the Middle East and terrorism, the decline of America and the rise of China, economic boom and bust, and corporate greed grab headlines around the world. However, there are few issues that divide society like the death penalty.

Martin Jones, a former anti-death penalty campaigner and human rights lawyer, encompasses the issue well. Jones had worked with a famous London-based human rights organization for more than a decade, touring the world documenting instances of the death penalty. He believed he was 'fighting the good fight'. "I had dedicated my life to **eradicating** the death penalty," he said. All that changed on January 24, 2009.

Jones returned home from a business trip to Myanmar, Singapore, and Malaysia to find his home **ransacked** and his wife, Mary, and their infant son, Harry, slain.

"Then and there I faced a crisis of **conscience**," Jones said. "How could I **reconcile** my beliefs with what had happened to my family?"

Jones's self-doubt was further compounded several days later when two fifteen-year-old boys were arrested for the murders. Because the boys are under the age of 18, they can only be tried as **minors**, and if found guilty, they will still probably be released on their 21ˢᵗ birthdays. Even if the boys were adults, there is no provision in England for the death penalty.

"The logical, reasonable part of me thinks they should be imprisoned for the rest of their **miserable** lives," Jones said. "In my heart, I want to see them hang."

In England, as part of the **European Union**, the use of the death penalty is prohibited.

Martin Jones's case is extreme. However, in recent years, there has been a **groundswell** of support for the death penalty in countries that do not practice capital punishment. This has alarmed leading human rights organizations which worry the introduction of capital punishment could lead to the *brutalizing effect*.

According to leading anti-death penalty campaigner, Jisu Kim, the death penalty has a brutalizing or **coarsening** effect either upon society or those officials and jurors involved in a criminal justice system which imposes it.

"There is clear evidence proving in countries where capital punishment is practiced that such a sentence is responsible for increasing murder rates," Ms. Kim said. "It sends a message to people that it is acceptable to kill in some instances, and that society has scant regard for the **sanctity** of life."

Either way, the heated debate surrounding the death penalty is not about to go away soon.

Comprehension Questions

1. Who is Martin Jones?
2. What was his opinion on the death penalty, and how did it change?
3. In what circumstances can the death penalty be handed down in England?
4. What does the "brutalizing effect" refer to?
5. What is meant by the "sanctity of life"?

Discussion Questions

1. Should the state be able to take a citizen's life? Explain.
2. How would you react if someone close to you was murdered?
3. How would you feel if someone close to you was sentenced to death?
4. What are some of the key problems of the death penalty?
5. What are some of the strengths of capital punishment?
6. Is capital punishment really a deterrent for crime?
7. What crimes, if any, should the death penalty be applied to?
8. Why do you think there are more men than women on death row?
9. Should the death penalty be applied to minors? Why or why not?
10. Do you think that a prison sentence is enough to rehabilitate a murderer?

Notes

Techniques
Section

What is body language?

Your body can do many things. Did you know that your body can even talk? It is true. Your body is able to communicate with other people, and you do not even need to use your voice to say anything! Body language includes gestures and facial expressions.

Why do we use body language?

As was just mentioned, we use body language, hand gestures, and facial expressions to communicate our thoughts, feelings, and ideas. If you think that the deaf or hearing-impaired are the only people who rely on their hands and bodies to talk, then you are wrong! We all constantly move our bodies and hands to express ourselves. It is a natural part of communication. For example, when you meet your friends and converse, do you just stand still and avoid moving? If you do, your friends might think you are not feeling well, or they may think you are acting strange, and that is because you are.

Video

Watch the videos, and answer the following questions.

1. How do the presenters express themselves non-verbally?
2. Which presenter seems more controlled, focused, and engaging? Why?
3. What do you consider to be effective body language?

What to Do

Feel Free to Move

Just because there is a podium in front of your audience does not mean you have to stand behind it at all times. You are giving a presentation, not a formal speech. Get away from the podium, and walk around. Communicate with the audience with not only your voice but with your entire body as well. Use your hands, arms, head, torso, and legs.

Be Yourself

When using body language, it is important to be natural. Do not use body language that seems odd or uncomfortable to you. You will inevitably look strange. Instead be yourself, and use body language that you would normally use.

Set the Mood

Your body language communicates volumes to your audience. Use it to set the mood of your presentation. If you are discussing a serious topic, then you will want to express the gravity of the issue by using sharp, crisp movements. If you you are presenting a humorous topic, then you will express the lightness of the issue by using large, exaggerated movements.

Move Deliberately

As mentioned above, it is okay to move around in front of your audience. Walk around the stage or platform. Pace back and forth if you want, but make sure that every movement has a purpose. You must move with deliberate intention. Each movement must be caluclated and have purpose. If you move erractically or without a purpose, you will look odd and unprepared.

Body Language to Avoid

Slouching	If you bend forward and your shoulders are drooping, then you are slouching. This body language makes you look tired, bored, and unsure of yourself. Always stand with your back straight and chest out, and then you will look confident and composed.
Crossing Your Arms	When do your parents cross their arms? They probably do this when they are angry. Crossing your arms is considered closed body language. It sends a negative signal to the audience that you are not interested in speaking or engaging them.
Putting Your Hands on Your Hips	Placing your hands on your hips is unnatural. Who does this? Models do this, but you are not a model; you are a presenter. Placing your hands on your hips makes you look too assertive; use your hands to communicate.
Putting Your Arms behind Your Back	Your hands are tools for communicating, and if you put them behind your back, you are intentionally avoiding communication with the audience, not to mention looking too casual and tired. This also gives the impression you are hiding something.
Putting Your Hands in Your Pockets	Placing your hands in your pockets is a big no-no. Have you ever seen salespeople try to sell you something while they had their hands in their pockets? Probably not because salespeople realize that people usually interpret "hands in pockets" as a sign of untrustworthiness and deceitfulness.
Touching Your Face, Hair, or Mouth	Do not fidget. Do not touch your face. This makes you look nervous, silly, and uncomfortable. Also, do not play with your hair. This makes you look unintelligent and shy. Finally, do not touch your mouth. This is bad because if you place your hand over your mouth, you will muffle your voice.
Rocking and Swaying	Rocking your body back and forth and swaying from side-to-side are bad for your presentation. These awkward movements make you look nervous, unprepared, and uncomfortable. Instead, stand still or walk slowly, deliberately, and confidently.
Repetitive Gestures	It is important to use a variety of gestures throughout your presentation since this will make you appear comfortable, natural, and in control; whereas, using the same gesture over and over again will have the opposite effect.

Gestures

Gestures are how we communicate using our hands. When we present, all too often we become self-conscious, and the question we often ask ourselves when making a presentation is, "What do I do with my hands?" As pointed out earlier in this chapter, we should not fold them under our arms, we should not hide them behind our backs, and we should not put them in our pockets. The question remains, "Where do they go?" In longer, more detailed presentations, your hands might be busy with cue cards or a remote control for the slideshow. This does not mean you can hide them away when they are not in use. Again, think about how you communicate with your friends or family when you are talking with them about something.

Exercise: Put Your Hands Up

Find a partner. Using the list of twenty situations listed below, take turns acting these out using only hand gestures. Do not speak or point to the sentences in the book.

1. There is no love between us anymore.
2. I don't find that very funny.
3. Where is that terrible smell coming from?
4. Do you understand?
5. Can I borrow 20 million won?
6. Your boyfriend/girlfriend is very attractive.
7. Where is my mobile phone?
8. You are late again.
9. You decide what we should have for dinner.
10. Look at that really tall guy!
11. Have you been drinking?
12. Congratulations, you did it!
13. Did you hear about the famous sports star that was caught cheating?
14. I paid last time. It's your turn.
15. I want a perm like that guy!
16. I think he has been lying to you.
17. Slow down! There is no need to be in a hurry.
18. You look great in that t-shirt.
19. Wow! What an awesome surprise.
20. Did you step in gum?

Facial Expressions

Body language is more than the way we move and what we do with our hands. A lot of what we are trying to communicate, or not communicate, can be seen on our faces. Make no mistake: you might be delivering the most interesting content there is, with the boldest and most exciting movements and gestures, but if you are not interested in your topic, it will show on your face. Why? Facial expressions are innate, and this means they are a part of who we are, and they cannot always be learned or unlearned. Does this mean you should give up on trying to control your facial expressions? Absolutely not!

If you want to harness your face and what it tells the world, it is important to first have an interest in what you are presenting. Be passionate, and care about your topic. If you are not interested in the information you are sharing, go back to the beginning, and ask yourself what is the purpose of your presentation.

Finally, do not over-practice facial expressions. If you think too much about this, there is a chance you could come across as waxy and wooden, which can be humorous, but also highly inappropriate.

Exercise: Let's Face It

Show your partner the facial expression you would use after experiencing the following:

1. Unexpectedly, your English teacher orders you to write a five page essay before next class.
2. Your best friend tells you they are part of a campus couple.
3. A drunk vomits on your new shoes while you are riding on the subway.
4. Your mother tells you an unknown distant relative has left your family US$2,000,000.
5. You get your score back from your exam, but you are sure your teacher has made an error grading your paper.
6. You are supposed to meet your friend at Gangnam Station at 5 p.m., but they do not show up until 6:30 p.m.
7. You meet a friend in Hongdae only to discover they are wearing the same shirt, jeans, and sneakers as you.
8. Your family decides to move to New Zealand to spend more time playing golf.
9. Your father tells you there was a mix-up at the hospital after you were born, and you are not his child.
10. You find a wallet belonging to the mayor of Seoul.

Exercise: Bringing It Together

Now, it is time to combine all the aspects of body language you have covered in this chapter.

A class member will be selected to make a one-minute spontaneous presentation on a topic of the teacher's choice. After finishing, the student will select another classmate and topic for the next presentation. This will continue until every class member has presented.

When making your presentation, be sure to use body language. For this presentation, your style is much more important than the content. Use big gestures and contort your face, but, above all have fun and relax!

Possible Topics

1. You are a deer. Convince a bear to not eat you.

2. Explain three uses of a pen besides writing.

3. Convince us that water is harmful to our health.

4. You are a salesperson. Try to sell us the shoes you are wearing.

5. Explain three uses of a purse besides carrying things.

6. Explain three different ways to eat a hamburger.

7. Explain why gravity is inconvenient.

8. Give us three reasons why walking is unhealthy.

9. Explain why yellow dust is good.

10. Convince us of why we should eat insects.

11. Explain how to read a book without using your hands.

12. Explain three uses of a toothbrush besides brushing your teeth.

13. What are 3 things you can teach your instructor?

14. Convince us to wear sunglasses at night.

15. You are a salesperson. Try to sell your instructor to your classmates.

16. Convince us you are Miss Korea.

17. You are a tennis ball. Convince the tennis racket not to hit you.

18. Which actor or actress would portray you in a movie about your life and why?

19. Convince us that your imaginary friend is real.

20. You are a robot. Convince us to polish you.

Exercise: Applying Body Language to a Script

Below there are two short scripts. With a partner or in groups, read the scripts aloud. Every time you see a **boldfaced** word, use body language, gestures, or facial expressions to emphasize that word.

The Dangers of Secondhand Smoke

Secondhand smoke, also known as passive smoke, poses a **serious** health threat to people. There are **two** forms of this kind of smoke: side stream smoke that comes from the end of the cigarette and mainstream smoke that is actually **exhaled** by the smoker. Those who **breathe in** the secondhand smoke are exposed to the same **toxic** chemicals that are in tobacco products. **First**, it is estimated that about **3,400** non-smokers die of **lung** cancer because of secondhand smoke. Also, it can cause breathing problems like **coughing** and **chest discomfort**. Furthermore, secondhand smoke has increased the number of children who develop asthma. Finally, women, who are exposed to secondhand smoke, are at **greater** risk of having babies with **low** birthweights. In conclusion, secondhand smoke is **dangerous** to everyone, so it is **important** to **avoid** it always.

The Importance of Saving Money

Most people agree that **money** is a necessary and **important** part of our lives. **Why**? Money gives us the **power** to buy items that we need to live as well as things we want to have. However, what will you do in the **future** when you are **old** and retired? Instead of thinking about how to **spend** your next paycheck, why not **focus** on saving that money? There are **three** simple ways to start **saving** money for your future. **First**, you can **cut** your spending by not buying things you **do not** need. For example, you could make your own **coffee** instead of purchasing it at a cafe. **Second**, find hobbies that require **little** or **no** money. **Reading**, **hiking**, or **dancing** are some possible **low** cost alternatives. **Third**, make a budget, and **remember** to stick to it! If **you** follow these easy steps, **you** will be doing yourself a **huge** favor.

Exercise: Applying Body Language to a Script

Now, it is your turn. Below are two short scripts. Read the scripts, and <u>underline</u> words you consider important (descriptive words and actions). When you have finished, practice the script. Make sure to use body language, gestures, or facial expressions to emphasize the underlined words.

The Internet

Today, the Internet plays a vital role in all of our lives. As a matter of fact, most of you probably do not know what life was like without it. However, did you know that the Internet was first created by US scientists in the 1960s as a result of the Cold War with the USSR? It is true! Shortly after the launch of Sputnik, the US created the Defense Advanced Project Research Agency (DARPA). The original purpose of the Internet, or the Arpanet as it was called at that time, was to provide a communications network that would still operate even if part of the network were destroyed in a nuclear explosion. The basic idea was that if the most direct route or path connecting two computers were broken, then the information could be directed to other alternate paths through the use of a router. While the Internet was mainly used by scientists and the military, it evolved and developed during the next two decades, and by the early 1990s, the Internet became a household name with the creation of the World Wide Web by Sir Tim Berners-Lee.

Culture Shock Revisited

Have you ever heard of culture shock? I am sure most of you are familiar with this term. It refers to the surprising, jolting, and even unsettling feelings a person may experience when they travel to a new place and encounter a culture quite different from their own. However, do you know what reverse culture shock is? This is a phenomenon that affects some people who have either traveled abroad extensively or have lived overseas for a long period of time. When they return to their own country, they have difficulty assimilating back into their own culture. Unlike culture shock, most people do not expect to feel like a foreigner when they return home. People experiencing reverse culture shock might feel a range of emotions including boredom, confusion, frustration, restlessness, and alienation. Therefore, it is important to be aware of this phenomenon when you go abroad, so you can be prepared to readjust and reacquaint yourself to your surroundings when arriving back home.

What is your voice?

Your voice is the wonderful adaptation that allows you to converse with the world around you. By allowing air to travel from your lungs, through your windpipe vibrating your vocal cords, and finally escaping from your mouth, you are able to make noise. This "noise" is your voice, but your voice is actually much, much more than that. It is the tool that you use to communicate orally, but you also use it to convey meaning, express emotion, and emphasize ideas.

Often, it is not what you say that is important, but how you say it.

Why do we use our voice?

It should come as no surprise that you use your voice to communicate with others around you. However, as a means of communication, your voice conveys more than simply words. Your voice conveys your feelings and emotions, and it is vital to consider this when you are presenting.

For instance, if you are standing before the audience and ask them, "Are you all having a good day?", the intent of what you are saying is clear — "Are you well?" However, if you lengthen the emphasis on the vowel sound in the word *good* the meaning of the sentence changes completely.

"Are you all having a *goooood* day?" At best, what this actually means is, "Has your day been as difficult as mine?" At worst, it could mean something like, "I really hope you are having a miserable day." This form of communication lies at the heart of linguistic devices like irony and sarcasm.

In addition, volume has an impact on the way we present. If we increase the volume at strange times, we, again, run the risk of confusing the audience. Also, if we are too quiet, we run the risk of not being heard. The best advice is to be as natural as possible and practice, practice, practice!

Video

Watch the videos, and answer the following questions.

1. How does the first presenter sound? How about the second presenter?
2. Which presenter sounds more confident, informed, and prepared? Why?
3. How does your voice change when speaking to different people?

Problems to Avoid

Speaking Too Softly

When talking to people, you want to make sure you speak loudly enough, so everyone can hear you. However, some people have a tendency to speak quietly in front of an audience usually because they are nervous. If this sounds like you, you need to focus on projecting your voice.

Speaking Too Quickly

It is a natural reaction to increase our speaking speed when stressed, and since most people are afraid of speaking in front of an audience, you can easily see why this is such a big problem in many presentations. If you speak too quickly, your message will be lost since your audience will have difficulty following your speech. In order to correct this problem, prepare for your presentation well, and begin your presentation in a relaxed state of mind.

Speaking in a Monotone Voice

Mono means *one* and *tone* means *sound*, so a monotone voice is a voice with only one sound. This means that the pitch does not rise and fall naturally, but it remains the same as a person talks. Speaking in a monotone voice is very unnatural. Not only will you sound both bored and boring, but you will put your audience to sleep.

Mumbling

To mumble means to speak without moving your lips and enunciating words. Mumbling is problematic since your speech is muffled and is not clear. This will lead your audience to misunderstand or be unable to follow your presentation. In addition, mumbling is a sure sign that either you are extremely nervous, or you did not practice enough.

What to Do

Project Your Voice

If you want people in the back of the audience to hear you, you must project your voice. To do this, you need to breathe and speak from your diaphragm (located above your stomach). Place your hand on your stomach, and breathe in and out. If you feel your hand rise and fall, then you are breathing correctly. Avoid breathing and speaking from your chest since this will make your voice sound soft and weak.

Stress Important Words

When we want to emphasize an important word, we can place stress on it. There are several ways to do this. First, you can draw out the vowel sound longer when saying the word. Second, you can adjust the volume of your voice when saying the word: louder or softer. Finally, you can pause briefly before saying something important. This helps build a little suspense.

Read Aloud

Once you have a script, read it aloud. If there are important words, underline them and either use word stress, volume, or a pause to add emphasis. Once you have done this, continue reading your script aloud emphasizing the important words. It is good to read aloud to know how you sound. You can also record your voice and listen to it. Knowing how you sound helps you find areas to improve.

Use Emotional Emphasis

Our voice is a great tool for letting people know how we feel. If we just listen to someone's voice, without looking at that person, we can tell quite accurately if that person is having a good day or not. How do we use emotional emphasis? Imagine this. Someone is running across the street, and a car is about to hit them. Would you use a soft, happy voice to warn that person? Absolutely not! You would use a loud, cautious voice instead.

Exercise: Word Stress

It is important to know that stressing different words in the same sentence will change the implied meaning you want to convey. Look at this example:

Give me the blue pencil.

Without stressing any of the words, this statement would be understood as a simple request. However, if stress is placed on "me", then the sentence is emphasizing who and who not to give the pencil to. The sentence is no longer a request.

Give **me** the blue pencil.

In addition, if the stress is placed on "pencil", then the emphasis is on the specific object. Again, the sentence is expressing what object is or is not wanted by the speaker.

Give me the blue ***pencil***.

Now, stress different words in the sentences below by either changing your volume, drawing out the vowel sound, or pausing. How does the meaning change?

1. I did my homework.

2. She said she does not like you.

3. I will call you tomorrow.

4. Write your name on the top of the paper.

5. I will come home at 8 p.m.

6. Follow me into the store.

7. Listen to this story on the news.

8. Meet me at the restaurant tonight.

9. Don't touch the hot stove.

10. Find me a book to read.

Exercise: Applying Your Voice to a Script

Below there are two short scripts. With a partner or in groups, read the scripts aloud. When you see a **boldfaced** word, increase your volume. When the word is underlined, draw out the vowel sound. Finally, when you see "...", pause before continuing.

A Life-Changing Moment

Have you ever experienced a situation that has changed your life? ... When I was in high school, I took a class that **profoundly** altered my life, **but** actually, it was **not** the class that changed my life ... **rather** it was the teacher ... Mr. Gross. He was my history teacher and soon became ... my idol. Mr. Gross was an **exceptional** teacher who was able to reach out to students and make a **big** difference in their lives. As an **educator**, he was an amazing teacher who was known for his talent of bringing history ... to life. His lectures took the drab, boring subject and **turned** it into something interesting for students. Moreover, as a **person**, he was ... caring, ... thoughtful, and ... took a personal interest in the lives of his students. After taking his class, ... my life changed. ... From that time on, I **knew** that I wanted to become ... a teacher.

A New Face

When meeting people for the **first** time, we often look at their outward appearance, and before speaking to them, determine what kind of people they are. This is called ... stereotyping, and **although** most people would **deny** doing this, appearance plays a **very** important role ... in our lives. As a matter of fact, most of us have our own **primping** rituals to make us look our **best**. For example, we might do up our hair, or make up our faces, or make sure our clothes are color-coordinated, or **even** shine our shoes. All of these seemingly minor details are examples of how we try to change the **exterior** appearance of ... ourselves. **However**, ... for some it is not enough. These people take it a step further and decide to take drastic action: ... plastic surgery.

Exercise: Applying Your Voice to a Script

Now, it is your turn. Below there are two short scripts. Read the scripts and <u>underline</u> words you consider important. When you have finished, practice the script. Make sure to use your voice by either increasing the volume, drawing out the vowel sound, or pausing to emphasize the underlined words.

The Price of Love

For most of us, our freshman year is a year of firsts. It can be the first time we have had the freedom to do what we want to do when we want to do it. Our freshman year can also be a time of first love. We meet that special someone in a class, and one thing leads to another. Before you know it, you are one half of a campus couple. For a while the relationship is fun and exciting. You get to attend the same classes, look into one another's eyes instead of focusing on the lecturer. Mid-terms come and go, and the results are terrible. After the exams, your friends start pestering you to spend time with them. You cannot because you are worried about offending your lover. You start to resent that person and see them as an inconvenience. A week or two later, you finally decide to claim back your independence. However, it is too late. Your GPA is in ruins, and your friends have abandoned you. This is exactly what happened to my sister.

I Want to Ride My Bicycle

As a child, I fell in love with my bicycle. My bicycle gave me my first taste of independence. I could cover distances far greater than I could on foot. I was able to visit new places and experience new things on my own terms. The years have passed, and things have changed. These days, I find myself inside, chained to a desk focusing on study: nothing but study. On my way home from campus a few weeks ago, I passed by a cycle shop. In the window was a gleaming new mountain bike. It was expensive, but I wanted it. I had some money saved from my vacation job, so I decided to buy it. The next day, I mounted my new bike and cycled to my university. It was horrible. I thought I was going to die. After I arrived at school, I locked my bike up and went to class. A few hours later I returned to find my new bike had been stolen. I then realized my childhood was over, and it was time for me to accept the realities of being an adult.

Exercise: Using Emotional Emphasis

Read the following sentences aloud. Make sure to use the appropriate emotional emphasis as you practice.

1. Students are strongly discouraged from using the elevator between 9 a.m. and 5 p.m.

2. Before you get on the train, make sure you kiss your grandmother goodbye.

3. I can't believe I failed the mid-term exam. It's not my fault!

4. Move your car! I'm in a hurry!

5. I feel really sleepy, and I'm really hungry.

6. Yes! We finally won! It took a long time, but it finally happened.

7. You know you are not allowed in here. Get out now!

8. Wow! That really tasted great.

9. No, I don't want to eat pizza again. I prefer steamed fish and broccoli.

10. I'd prefer it if you put the camera away.

11. I've got to get it. What a bargain!

12. Take a left and then a right. At the end of the street, you'll see the fire station.

13. I wish I was five centimeters taller.

14. No more food for me; I've had enough to eat.

15. I saw a terrible accident on the way here today.

16. Good news! The test results were negative.

17. Have you seen my wallet?

18. Get down on the floor. This is a robbery!

19. Well, I guess I should have studied harder if I had wanted to pass that test.

20. I hate rush hour traffic.

What to Do

One of the key aspects of a great presentation is being able to connect with your audience. As we already know, we communicate a huge amount using our voices. One way to become closer to your audience is to be natural and relaxed. For example, when you are meeting your friends and talking to them, do you talk like a robot? Of course not!

Your voice tells the audience how you feel about what you are presenting. If your voice is flat, you probably do not really care for your topic. Conversely, if you are natural and relaxed, your audience is more likely to warm up to you.

Breathing

There are times when you are presenting, and you come to a complete stop. Your brain freezes. You lose the power of thought and communication. What do you do?

The answer sometimes lays in breathing. If you fail to breathe, you starve your brain of oxygen. When that happens, your brain fails to function, and you can become glued to the spot. The same applies to your voice and eye contact. To be natural and relaxed, make sure you are pausing and taking breaths regularly.

For example, stand up and repeat the following sentences in one breath:

Buckets of blue bug's blood. Buckets of blue bug's blood. Buckets of blue bug's blood. Buckets of blue bug's blood.

You probably noticed that your voice sped up towards the end as you started to run out of oxygen. Also, in terms of your body language, you probably found that you were not moving. Maybe you felt tightness in your forearms and shoulders.

Now, try the same thing again. However, this time breathe between the sentences and relax your arms and shoulders.

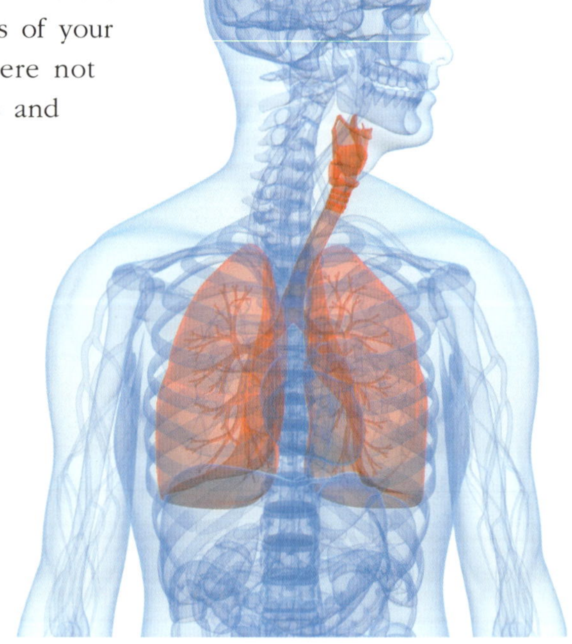

What is eye contact?

Think about the last time you talked with someone. Maybe this morning you had a simple conversation with your parents over breakfast or discussed your homework with your classmates before class. How did you talk to these people? Did you look at the floor, or the ceiling, or at something else other than the person you were talking to? I doubt it. You probably looked them straight in the eyes as you spoke with them. This is eye contact: looking at people when you talk to them.

Why do we use eye contact?

The simplest and most logical answer is that you do this because it is how you naturally communicate with people. Moreover, in a presentation, eye contact is necessary for several reasons.

First, it shows that you are well prepared and know what you are talking about. If people know their topics well, then they can talk about them without the need of reading from a script or having to rely on notes. Being able to present and maintain eye contact shows the audience you have taken the time to practice and prepare, and you will gain the audience's respect.

Second, eye contact personalizes the relationship between you and the audience. It is an easy way to engage the audience and communicate with them. Looking at someone when you talk to them shows you are interested in them or at least interested in communicating with them. Have you ever had a professor lecture a class from notes, never looking up at the students? How did you feel: engaged and interested or alienated and disinterested? Most likely, it was the latter.

Third, you will appear more knowledgeable, trustworthy, and reliable. Have you ever seen a salesperson not look you in the eye when answering your questions about a product you want to buy? If you have, did you buy it? You probably did not since avoiding eye contact is a tell-tale sign that someone is lying.

Video

Watch the videos, and answer the following questions.

1. What is the first presenter looking at? How about the second presenter?
2. Which presenter seems more comfortable, believable, and natural? Why?
3. How important is it to look at people when speaking to them?

Knowledge vs Memorization

Often when speakers think about maintaining eye contact with the audience, they are overwhelmed with the fear of forgetting what they want to say, so they feel obligated to memorize their entire presentation, thus avoiding the need to read from a script and allowing them to focus on the audience.

Unfortunately, this is probably the worst approach you can take because memorization is not knowledge. If you memorize information for a test, do you really know that information, did you learn it, and will you remember the details after you have taken the test? Of course not. Committing the information to your short-term memory without ever understanding or knowing that information is not knowledge.

If you memorize your presentation, you are putting yourself at greater risk of forgetting what you want to say because you are simply memorizing the order of the presentation's content. Therefore, if you memorize the order, but you forget one part of that order, will you be able to remember the information after that one point you forgot? The answer is most likely "no".

Therefore, what can you do? First, avoid rote memorization of your presentation, and instead, focus on actually learning what you want to say. Do you have to memorize or read from a script to tell someone about your hobby or your favorite teacher? Of course not. You already know this information. You do not need to memorize it. However, how do you do this with a topic you are not familiar with? Honestly, there is no short-cut or easy way to learn the information and become comfortable presenting it. The answer is: practice, practice, practice.

However, despite practicing, how do you prepare for a situation in which you simply go blank and forget what you want to say? Answer: use cue cards. Are you expected to memorize your presentation? Absolutely not! Are you expected to know your presentation? Of course!

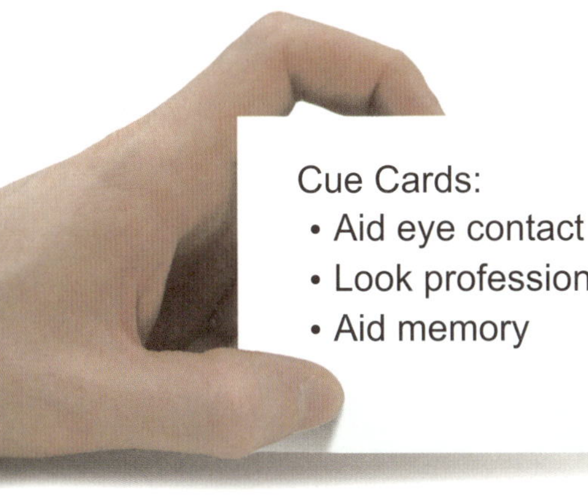

Cue Cards:
- Aid eye contact
- Look professional
- Aid memory

Cue Cards:
- Small, thick paper
- Easy to hold
- Do not make noise

Cue Cards:
- Come in many sizes
- Should be no larger
  than 10 X 15 cm

Cue Cards:
- Do not need to read
  a script
- Do not memorize
  everything

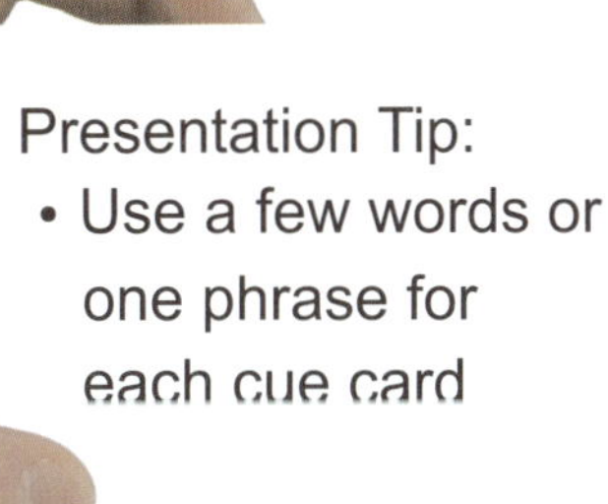

Presentation Tip:
- Use a few words or
  one phrase for
  each cue card

Exercise: Impromptu Presentations

Below there are some topics you are already familiar with. Choose one, and without writing a script, prepare a brief presentation based on only what you already know about the topic. If you need cue cards, use the templates provided at the bottom of the page.

• My family	• My pet
• My favorite vacation	• My favorite day of the week
• My dream job	• My best friend
• My hometown	• My favorite restaurant
• My high school	• My hobby
• My favorite movie star	• My idol
• My least favorite holiday	• My biggest pet peeve
• My happiest memory	• My most challenging experience

Connecting with the Audience

We already know making eye contact in presentations is essential if you are to connect with your audience. However, when we are standing in front of 20, 200, 2000, or 20,000 people, how can we make eye contact effectively?

Clearly, we cannot hope to look every person in the eye. On the other hand, if you only focus on one or two people in the audience, you run the risk of making those people feel very uncomfortable and run the risk of alienating the rest of the audience.

At some point, you have probably all experienced the immense discomfort that comes with having a teacher or professor focus on you - and no one else - while they are teaching or lecturing. The only thing which goes through your mind in such a situation is, "Oh no! Why are you looking at me? Please, don't ask me a question!"

What is the solution?

When you stand before your audience, separate the audience into three groups in your mind: left, center, and right. As you give your presentation, scan between the different groups, being sure not to spend more than about five seconds looking at one person.

Be sure not to linger on one person for too long, but also avoid scanning too quickly back and forth across the audience. It will result in you giving your audience the impression you are watching a tennis match, and this can be very distracting for your audience. Also, you will appear nervous and ill-prepared. Remember, it is not necessary to make eye contact with every member of the audience.

Exercise: Look at Us

Choose one of the following topics, and, without cue cards, stand up and present on that topic to your audience. Make sure to practice using the aforementioned techniques.

A time you were sick	A food you like to cook	A time you were scared
A sport you enjoy	A season you prefer	A musician or artist you admire
A special gift you received	A place you like to visit	A goal you achieved

Checklist

Eye Contact	
Uses cue cards	· well · but reads sometimes · but reads a lot
Maintains eye contact	· with the entire audience · with most of the audience · with some of the audience · with none of the audience

Voice	
Uses emotional emphasis	☐ well ☐ at times ☐ never
Uses word stress	☐ well ☐ at times ☐ never

Speaks **coherently / incoherently**

Speaks **slowly / quickly**

Speaks **loudly / quietly**

Enunciates **well / poorly**

Body Language	
Uses hand gestures	☐ well ☐ at times ☐ never
Uses facial expressions	☐ well ☐ at times ☐ never

Moves around **deliberately / erratically**

Body language **sets / does not set** the mood

Body language is **varied / lacking**

Body language is **natural / rehearsed**

What are visual aids?

Visual aids, or visuals, are important tools for communicating well during presentations. They can encompass many things: PowerPoint slides, pictures, posters, charts, diagrams, graphs, and tangible objects are all visual aids. The verb form of *visual* is *visualize*, which means *make something able to be seen*, so visuals are anything that we can see with our eyes.

Why do we use visual aids?

Out of all of our five senses - sight, hearing, smell, touch, and taste - we rely most heavily on our sense of sight to gather information about the world around us. Close your eyes, and imagine you are unable to see. Relying only on your other four senses, how much of what is going on around you do you understand? Probably not much, and that is because we are visual creatures.

Video

Watch the videos, and answer the following questions.

1. What are the noticeable differences between the two presenters' visual aids?
2. Which presenter's visuals were easier to see, more meaningful, and more stimulating?
3. What do you think 'A picture is worth a thousand words' means?

Exercise: Test Your Visual Knowledge

Read the following statements, and answer true or false.

1. My audience should focus on my visuals more than on me. They are the presentation, not me.	T/F
2. It is okay to read from my visual aids.	T/F
3. My visual aid should be self-explanatory, so I do not need to point to it or explain it in detail.	T/F
4. It is okay if what I am saying does not correspond to what is on my current PowerPoint slide.	T/F
5. It is okay if I have my back turned to the audience.	T/F
6. I should include all the information and details on my PowerPoint slides.	T/F
7. Using a lot of text on my PowerPoint slides is good since my audience can read them.	T/F
8. A few spelling mistakes or typos are allowable since English is not my native language.	T/F
9. The more colors on the PowerPoint slide, the better.	T/F
10. The more detail and information on the slide, the better.	T/F
11. All of my slides do not need to support my presentation's main idea.	T/F
12. PowerPoint is the only visual aid that should be used in presentations.	T/F

Guidelines for Using Visuals

When using visual aids always remember the 3 Ps: *Point, Pivot,* and *Present.*

Point to the important information on the visual aids. (It is okay to look at your visual aids briefly as you do this.)
Pivot your head and body, so you are facing your audience again.
Present to your audience, not to the wall, ceiling, or visual aids.

Guidelines for Making Visuals

Color Contrast

Make sure the text color does not blend into the background color and the font is easy to read.

Why do presenters make their presentations an eye exam for those sitting in the back of the audience?

Use 30 Point Font

Make sure the text is large enough to read.

Why do people insist on filling all of the space with text? Using fewer words is more effective, meaningful, and powerful. Also, less text is easier to follow and understand.

Use few words

Fewer words make a bigger impact.

Guidelines for Making Visuals

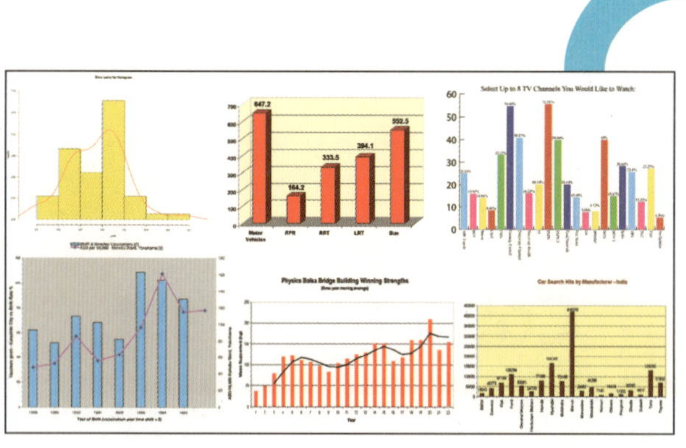

Do not put all the information on one slide. Use as many slides as you need.

Avoid using too many colors and colors that do not work well together.

Typos and misspelled words are obvious to the audience.

112

Symbols, Images, Words, and Your Brain

Your brain is divided into two halves. These halves are called lobes: the right lobe and the left lobe. Both process different information. The left side of the brain is logical and detail-oriented. It perceives patterns and order, and it recognizes words and language. On the other hand, the right side is philosophical and imaginative. It can believe and have faith in the unknown, and it recognizes symbols and images.

Connecting the two halves is a very thin membrane called the hypothalamus that acts as a bridge allowing information to pass between both lobes. If one side of the brain receives too much information, this will cause a small traffic jam at the hypothalamus (bridge), and the brain will have difficulty interpreting, understanding, and processing the information.

For example, if your visual aid has a lot of text, and you speak to the audience, the audience will need to both read and listen. Essentially, they will have a difficult time processing the information since the left sides of their brains will be working in overdrive. Soon their brains will overheat and shut down. Then, they will not pay attention. This situation is bad because once you lose the audience's attention, it is very difficult to get it back again.

In order to present your information clearly and use your visuals effectively, you must provide information for both sides of the brain. For example, use some charts, graphs, and data for your left lobe, but make sure to use symbols and images for the right lobe. When used together, your visuals will be powerful, and your message will stick.

Exercise: Symbols I

Match the following symbols to their appropriate meanings.

1. ♥	· The Heavens
2. ☠	· Christianity
3. 🕊	· Buddhism
4. ♣	· Love
5. ✝	· Luck
6. ★	· Peace
7. 卍	· Equality
8. ☾	· Death
9. ⚖	· Happiness
10. ☺	· Islam

Exercise: Symbols II

In small groups, discuss the following topics. What symbols or images do you think could be used to express them clearly?

Longevity	Peace	Love
Retirement	Happiness	Complex
Sadness	Marriage	Beauty
Knowledge	Weakness	Disagreement
Divorce	Investment	Security
Danger	Humor	Hatred
Boredom	Disgust	Failure
Success	Strength	Intelligence

Exercise: Symbols III

Use the boxes below to sketch a symbol or image you might use for the given topic. Try to be creative, but make sure it is clearly related to the topic. When finished, compare with a classmate.

Korean Culture

Final Exams

Smoking

Dating

What is your audience?

Why do we present? What is the significance? Your motivation in presenting is to communicate your wonderful, valuable, and meaningful ideas to other people. Those people are your *audience*. They are the ones that you will either be informing or persuading; therefore, it is necessary to get your ideas across clearly and effectively.

Why is your audience important?

Your audience is important because they are the ones who will receive your message. They might influence people like your boss or professor, so you must really focus and find more information about them. You need to think about who your audience is, and what is going to be informative, interesting, and new for them. If you forget your audience, stay home.

Video

Watch the following video clip of a question and answer session following a presentation.

1. In the first example, how could the question be improved?
2. In the second example, how would you have answered the question?
3. In the third example, how did the presenter handle the question?

Exercise: Matching Activity

Match the following people with the topic that you think best suits them.

High school girls	Overcoming Substance Addiction
University biology professors	Executive Management Strategies
Online game addicts	The Life and Times of Edmund Hillary
Shoe salespeople	What You Do Not Know about Taekwondo Robots
Cattle farmers	Seoul City Shortcuts
Retired golfers	How to Become a Success
Housewives	How to Dress Like an Idol
Taxi drivers	The Best Way to Remove Ink from Your Clothing
Businesspeople	Overcoming Racism in the Workplace
Mountain climbers	Understanding the Beef Price Index
English teachers	Photosynthesis: Keeping It Green
Five-year-old girls	Dealing with Unpleasant Odors
Five-year-old boys	Making the Most of the Company Dinner
CEOs	Keeping that Swing throughout the Golden Years
Homeless families	How to Handle Soju Parties
Freshman university students	An Alternative Approach to Religious Study
Smokers	Understanding Culture in the Classroom
Church-goers	Where to Turn when Life Turns on You
Foreign factory workers	Ways to Balance the Family Budget
Squid fishermen	Learn about Barbie and Friends

Exercise: Taboo Topics

When you are presenting, it is important to avoid unintentionally provoking or upsetting your audience. There are certain topics that are taboo among certain audiences. Central to this is knowing what not to present.

The following is a list of inappropriately matched audiences and topics. Choose one of the following, and make a short impromptu presentation on why this is a bad topic for the given audience.

1. You are planning to make a presentation on the best places to go in Hongdae for your grandmother and her friends.

2. You want to make a presentation on famous airplane crashes for flight attendants.

3. You want to make a presentation on why studying English is a complete waste of time for your English teacher.

4. You want to make a presentation on the futility of war to a group of weapons manufacturers.

5. You are planning on making a presentation to body builders on why a diet based on hamburgers is good.

6. You want to make a presentation on the benefits of kicking back and relaxing to high school seniors.

7. You are eager to present the topic, "Why all other universities are superior to your university" to your classmates.

8. You are planning on making a presentation to Canadian exchange students on there being no differences between them and Americans.

9. You want to make a presentation to environmentalists on the necessity of driving a car every day.

10. You have decided to talk to a group of elementary school students on the importance of planning for retirement.

Exercise: Creating Appropriate Topics

List three possible appropriate topics for each of the following groups.

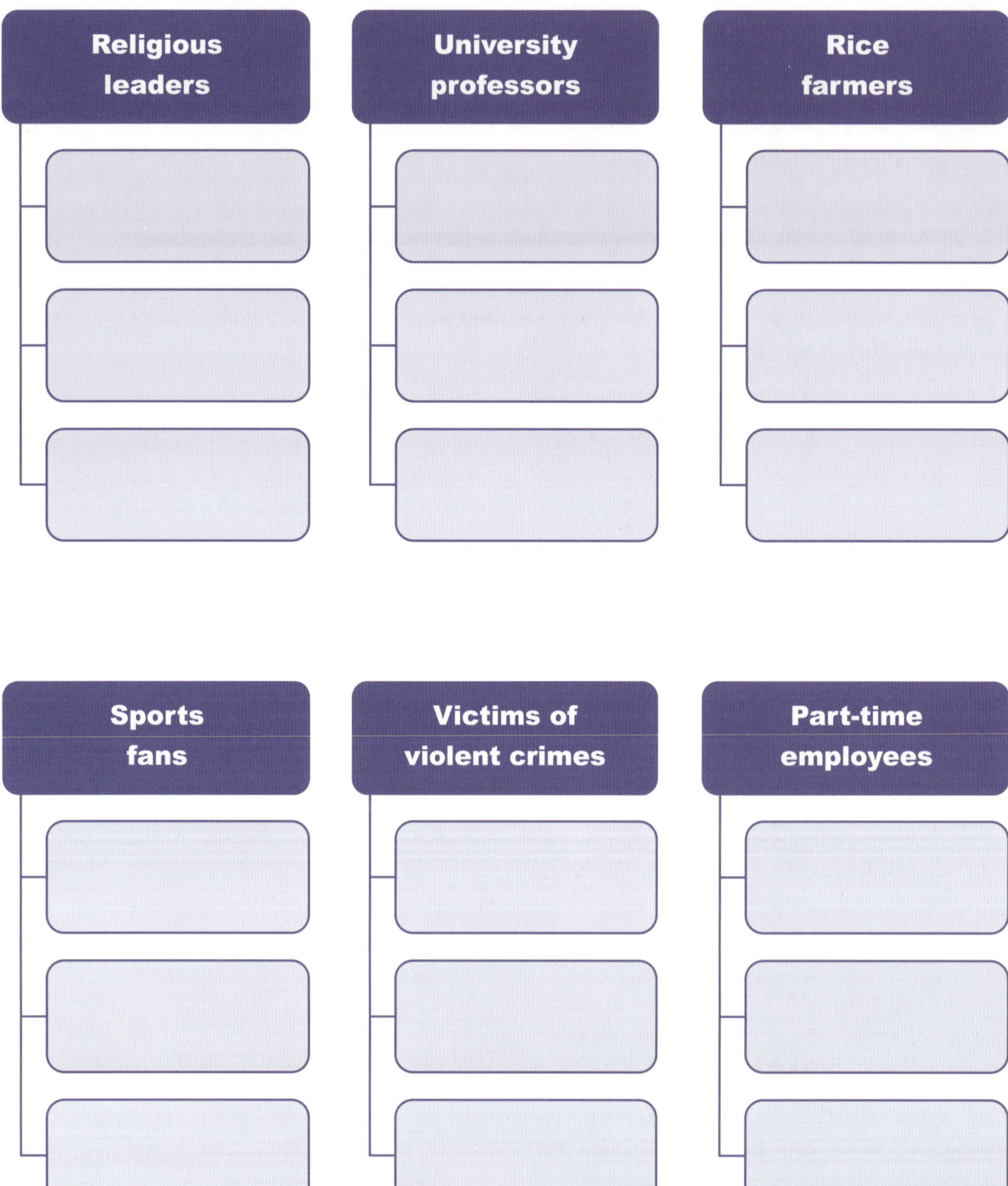

Handling Questions

Before, during, and/or after many presentations you will be required to field questions. At the beginning of your presentation, make sure you tell your audience when it is appropriate and inappropriate to ask questions. This will help you avoid losing the flow of your presentation through unsolicited questions, and it also gives you, the presenter, an opportunity to be mentally prepared to deal with such questions. Furthermore, when answering questions, there is an appropriate and inappropriate way to answer.

Inappropriate

Question: *I noticed you used the example of Singapore in your presentation. Are there any other Asian countries that use a similar system of conscription?*

Answer: *Singapore has two close neighbors, Malaysia and Indonesia. For the most part, relations between the countries have been okay... Umm, what was your question?*

It is clear from this example the presenter either misheard the question or simply failed to understand it. To avoid the potential embarrassment that comes with the example situation, follow these steps.

Appropriate

Question: *I noticed you used the example of Singapore in your presentation. Are there any other Asian countries that use a similar system of conscription?*

Step 1 Thank the audience member for their question.
Thank you Jeong-u. That is an interesting question.

Step 2 Repeat the question. This helps ensure you have understood the question, and it gives the audience a second chance to hear the question.
Your question is, are there any other Asian countries that use a similar system of conscription aside from Singapore?

Step 3 Answer the question.
Yes, there are other Asian countries that use the same system. Taiwan followed the Singaporean example, and Malaysia is seriously considering the idea.

Step 4 Seek affirmation.
Does that answer your question? Thank you, next question please.

Exercise: Responding to Questions

In pairs, take turns asking one of the following questions and giving appropriate answers.

1. Do you enjoy the crisp taste of *soju*?
2. What is the most difficult part of freshman life?
3. What do you imagine your life will be like in ten years?
4. Have you seen any good movies recently?
5. What was your worst dining experience?
6. Is global warming a reality?
7. Do you think body builders are attractive?
8. Why is pop music so unimaginative?
9. Should professors be able to wear jeans and t-shirts at work?
10. Why is a cup of coffee so expensive?

Dealing with Inappropriate Questions

Occasionally an audience member will ask an inappropriate question. The question may be genuine but misled, or the person might be a heckler.

Example

The presenter is making a presentation on the future relations between North Korea and South Korea.

Question: *Hey, great presentation! I really learned a lot about the future of the Korean Peninsula. Where did you get those shoes, and can I get your phone number?*

Good Answer: *My presentation was on the future of North and South Korean relations. I do not see what my shoes have to do with that. And no, you cannot have my number.*

Remember, when you are presenting, you are the boss. You control the room. You call the shots. Do not let yourself become derailed by inappropriate questions. If you think a question is irrelevant or rude, let the audience know.

Be Prepared

Becoming a good presenter is a long and often complex process. First, you need to understand the content of your presentation. This includes the structure, organization, and type of presentation. You also need to have a grasp of style: body language, eye contact, and voice. Imagine you have studied hard, and you have mastered content and style. Are you ready to present? Not quite. The following are a few things you need to know before you make your presentation.

Practice, Practice, Practice

It should come as no surprise that practicing your presentation is essential. However, if possible, practice with a friend. Rehearsing your presentation out loud gives you the opportunity to work on different aspects of voice, body language, and eye contact. It also enables you to correct the way you say hard-to-pronounce words.

A key benefit of presenting to a friend is you will have a more accurate idea of how your presentation will play out. When you practice your presentation in your head, it is always faster than if you were to present it out loud.

If you cannot find a friend to practice with, do not despair. Present out loud to a chair, desk, a family pet, or even while looking at yourself in the mirror. Ignore the shame of doing this. The benefits outweigh the consequences.

Know Your Surroundings

Many potentially good presentations have come undone because the presenters were not 100% familiar with their room. Before the audience arrives and you present, have a friend stand at the back of the room, and see if they can hear you from the front of the room.

On the day of your presentation, be sure to arrive five to ten minutes before beginning. Check and see if all the equipment you want to use in your presentation is working. This includes the computer, projector, audio, and video systems. This is your responsibility. If these things are not functioning properly, you will still be required to make your presentation.

If you are using PowerPoint, or another computer file in your presentation, save it on the computer before the beginning of the presentation. There is nothing worse than having to wait for presenters while they waste valuable time trying to access their presentation files from their USB or email. At the end of the presentation, you can delete the file.

Appendix
Section

What is Monroe's Motivated Sequence (MMS)?

MMS was created by Professor Alan Monroe and Professor Douglas Ehninger. Monroe and other researchers recognized that people seek balance in their lives. In other words, people want to feel harmony. Anything that disrupts their balance is a problem or a need. People naturally want to solve problems in order to regain balance. To solve problems, people take personal actions.

People are not always aware of the world's problems and solutions, so public speakers can use MMS to teach people about problems, solutions, and various actions the audience members should take.

When might we use MMS?

MMS can be used in presentations that call for changes in rules, laws, behaviors, actions, or other physical changes. Why? MMS describes a problem that requires a solution, and it calls the audience to do something. If your speech only persuades the audience members to change their opinions or thoughts, you cannot use MMS.

MMS is very personal to the audience. It involves logic and emotion. MMS is about explaining real-world problems, proposing real-world solutions, and telling the audience to take real-world actions.

Ask yourself these questions:
1. Is my opinion calling for a physical change in the real world?
2. Is there a real-world problem that I can make my audience care about?
3. Do I know a solution that will solve the problem?
4. Are there real-world things my audience can do right now to help solve the problem?

If you can answer "yes" to all of these questions, you can use MMS.

Video
Watch the following presentation, and answer the following questions.

1. What is the problem the presenter discusses?
2. What is the presenter's opinion?
3. What is the speaker's purpose in giving this presentation?
4. What is different about this presentation's structure compared to other presentations?

Step 1: Attention

The Attention Stage of MMS is very similar to other presentation introductions. There should be at least two main parts to the introduction:

Hook: Like any hook, there are many ways to get your audience's attention. Remember, MMS is about analyzing your audience. Whatever you say, make sure it is creative and relevant to your audience.

Your Opinion & Overview: Your opinion in MMS is the big solution you propose during the Satisfaction Stage. Here is an example opinion: *The university should sell Hyper Fuel energy drinks on campus.* You will restate your opinion many times in your presentation. Also, remember to give an overview of the main points which will be discussed in the Need, Satisfaction, and Visualization stages of MMS.

Example Attention Stage: Kim Minsu is a freshman at our university. Every day during lunch, Minsu walks down the long hill to local supermarkets to buy a drink. In the winter, Minsu is as cold as ice on his long trek. In the summer, he is hot and sweaty. Minsu misses out on exciting lunch discussions and valuable study sessions with his friends. There are other students like Minsu at our university. These students drink Hyper Fuel. The university should sell Hyper Fuel energy drinks on campus. I will cover three points. First, I will explain why not selling Hyper Fuel is bad for the university. Then, I will discuss how the university can get Hyper Fuel on campus. Finally, I will show the convenience and economical benefits of having Hyper Fuel here.

Exercise: Attention!

Make an outline using MMS. First, write your persuasive opinion statement:

____

Now, write your hook.

____

Finally, add an overview.

____

Now that you have captured the audience's attention, it is time to move on to the first main point of MMS: the Need Stage.

Step 2: Need

What is the real world problem that exists? Is it a problem in another country? Is it a problem in society? Is it a problem in the government? Is it a problem in your school? Is it a problem in your audience members' lives? There are two goals in the Need Stage of MMS:

Describe the problem using descriptive language. Once you describe the problem, you cannot go back to it later in the presentation. You must give all the necessary information about the problem in this part of your talk. Give evidence such as facts, statistics, expert opinions, and examples. This is a good place to use research and provide citations.

Make the audience care about the problem. To make the audience care about the problem, use emotion. Make them think about their lives, their families, their friends, their interests, their health, their happiness, their security, and other personal issues. This can be a big challenge if you choose a topic that is not relevant to your audience. It is easier to make your audience care about things happening in their town instead of trying to make your audience care about things happening in another country; however, it is possible to make your audience care about anything if you are an expert on the topic and you analyze your audience.

Example Need Stage: Students and faculty at our university do not have the freedom to purchase Hyper Fuel on our campus. Currently, the university does not have a contract with Hyper Fuel. In all campus buildings, there are numerous vending machines. None of these machines carry Hyper Fuel. None of our supermarkets are allowed to sell it, either. The university only sells water, soft drinks, and coffee. This creates a problem for students and faculty who drink healthy Hyper Fuel. Some people add to the weight of their bags by carrying Hyper Fuel to school each day. Unless they have access to a refrigerator, the drinks get warm and taste bad. Other students waste valuable time walking off campus to local supermarkets that sell Hyper Fuel. I have seen many of you leaving campus to buy drinks, and I have heard many of you complain about it. In addition to unhealthy choices, wasted time, and wasted energy, our university loses valuable income because people are spending money off-campus. This problem does not have to continue if we implement a very simple solution.

1. What are some of the descriptive words and images used to describe the problem?
2. What emotion does the speaker use to make you care about the problem?
3. What is your reaction? Why?

Exercise: Analyzing the Need

Continue making your outline by answering the following questions. Use the same opinion statement you wrote about in the Attention Stage.

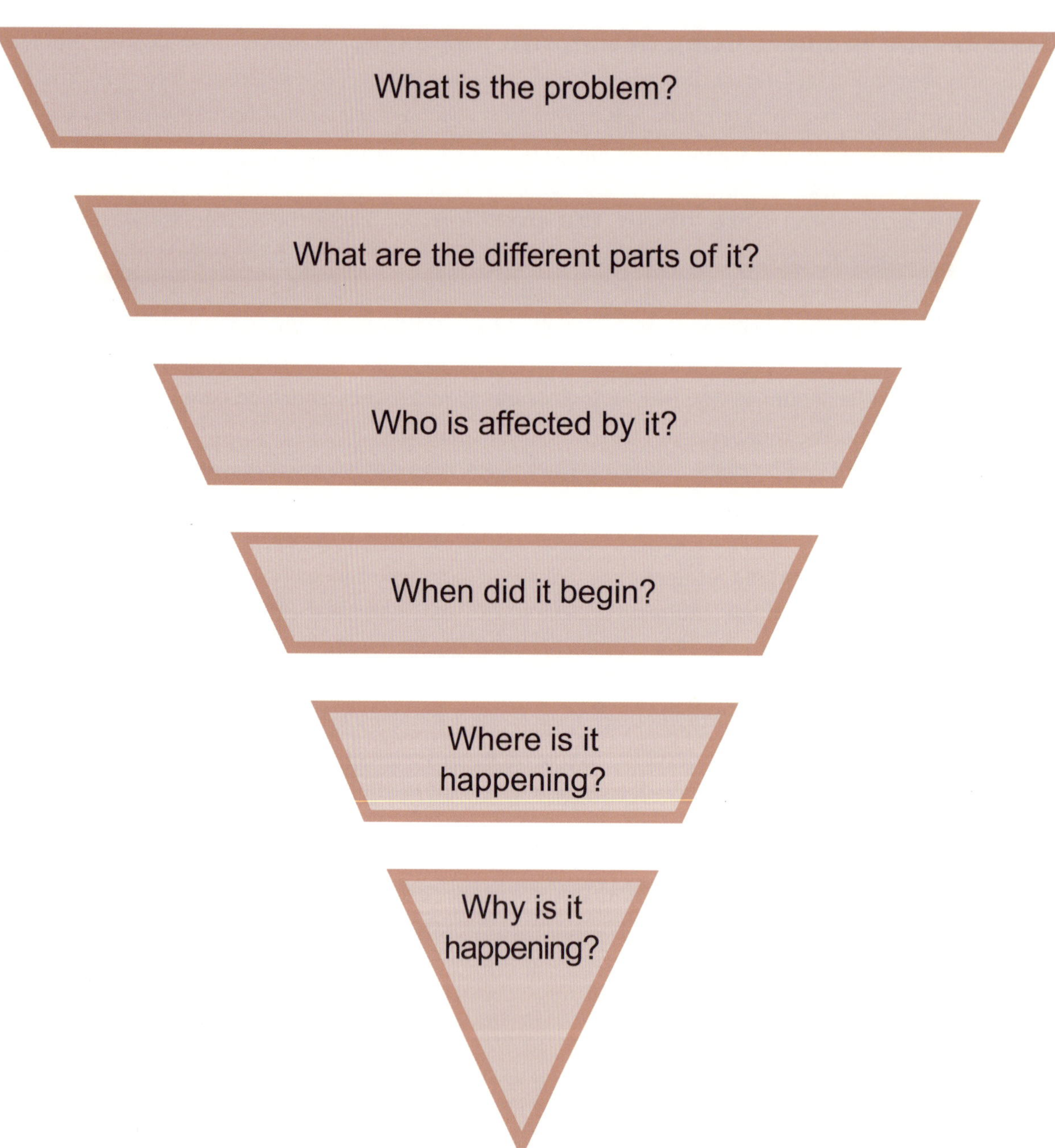

Now that your audience understands and cares about the problem, they will naturally want a solution. Give a transition sentence, and move on to the Satisfaction Stage.

Step 3: Satisfaction

This is the most challenging step of MMS. It requires you to propose a serious solution to the problem. Like an expert, you must be logical and creative in your solution. There are two goals in the Satisfaction Stage:

State a clear solution to the problem. Do this by restating your opinion statement. The opinion could be restated like this: *University officials should allow Hyper Fuel in vending machines and in shops on our campus.*

Explain the solution and all its parts in detail. When explaining your solution, you must be logical and specific. Think about the questions your audience might have: What? Who? When? Where? Why? How? Your audience wants to solve the problem, but they will only follow you if you give them a complete answer.

Some solutions are very easy to agree with. For example, most people would agree with this statement: The government should make the subway free for all citizens. Who should be in charge of this solution? When should it happen? The important thing to ask is **how** should the government make the subways free.

Your solution should be different from other possible solutions. There may be other ways to make the subway free for citizens. Explain to your audience that your way is the best way. You can also use a counterargument. Presentations that use MMS do not always need a counterargument, but sometimes it helps explain the solution.

Example Satisfaction (Solution) Stage: In order to make the university a better place, university officials should allow Hyper Fuel energy drinks to be sold on campus. It would be easy to get Hyper Fuel on campus. There is no doubt that the Hyper Fuel company would pounce on the chance to sell their products. First, the university officials should begin business discussions with Hyper Fuel. Next, a contract should be signed with Hyper Fuel allowing them to place vending machines on campus. Third, the supermarkets on campus should be notified that they can stock Hyper Fuel. By the end of the spring semester next year, Hyper Fuel could be all over campus. These types of business agreements happen all the time around the world. For example, at West University in the USA, university officials signed a contract with Hyper Fuel last year. They said the Hyper Fuel company was "terrific" to work with and supplied vending machines all over campus in just one day.

Exercise: Satisfy Me

Continue your outline by answering these questions regarding your solution to the problem.

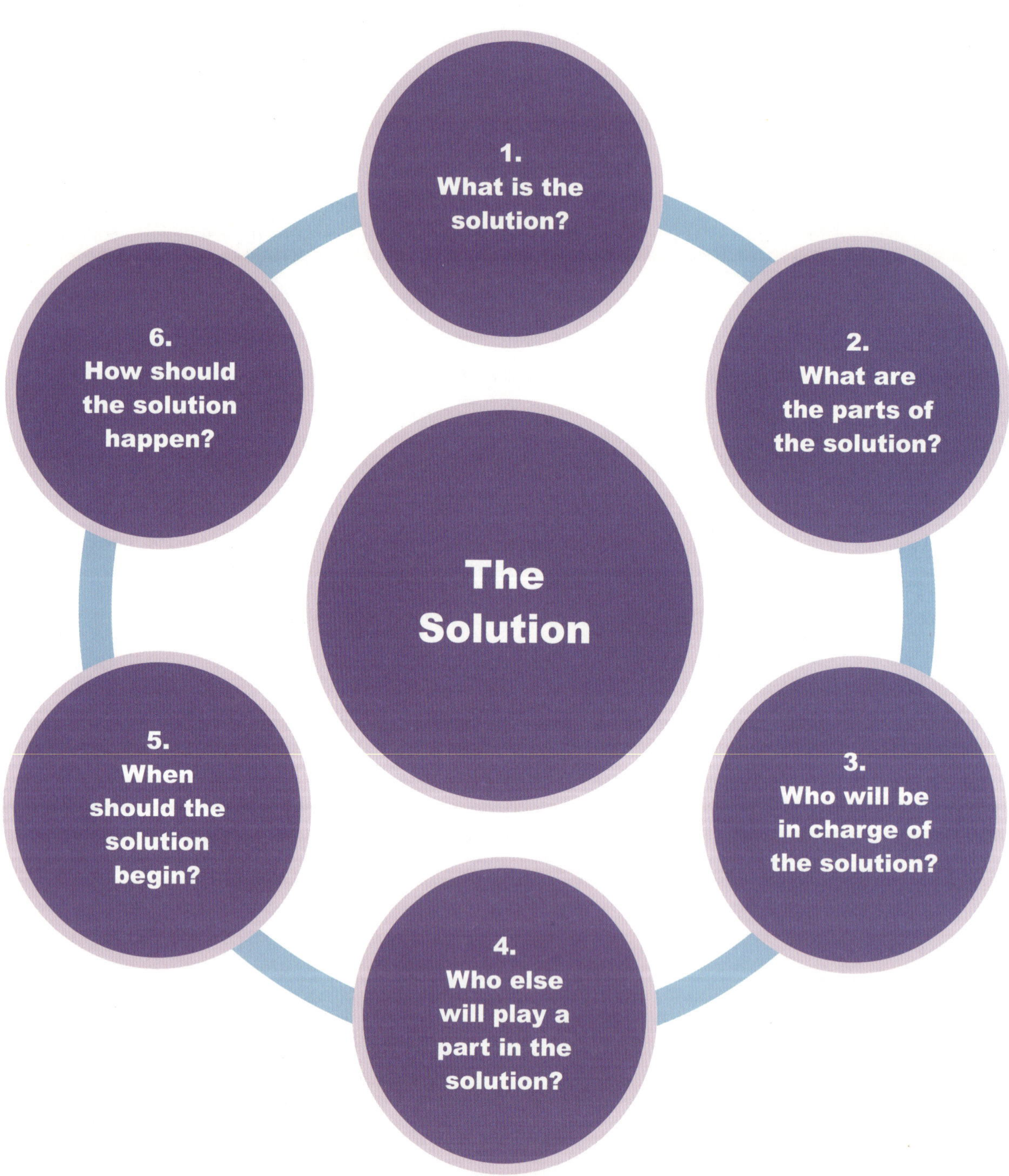

Step 4: Visualization

What will happen in the future after your solution is implemented? What will happen in the future if it is not? You must now give your expert opinion and describe future consequences. There are two goals in the Visualization Stage:

Describe the future consequences using emotion and descriptive language.
You have three methods to choose from when describing the future.

- **The positive method:** Use vivid imagery to describe all the future benefits that will happen.
- **The negative method:** Use vivid imagery to describe all the future problems and risks.
- **The combination method:** Use vivid imagery to describe both aspects.

Make the audience care about the future by playing to their emotions. You must analyze and involve your audience when talking about the future. How did you make them care about your problem in the Need Stage of MMS? Do the same thing in the Visualization Stage. Make them think about their lives, their families, their friends, their interests, their health, their happiness, their security, and other personal issues. Make them see and feel themselves in a future situation.

Example Visualization Stage: The benefits to having Hyper Fuel energy drinks at the university would be tremendous. The first benefit to having Hyper Fuel on campus relates to people like the student in my introduction, Kim Minsu. Students and faculty, who want Hyper Fuel, could walk outside of their classrooms or offices and easily find a vending machine filled with their favorite drink. There would be no more walking off campus or carrying around warm and weighty containers. The second benefit would be the money our university could make. For example, each department could collect a commission or percentage of sales on each Hyper Fuel energy drink sold. Another possibility would be money and free products supplied by the Hyper Fuel company if a contract is signed. Hyper Fuel often donates free drinks and snacks to universities around the world. More importantly, they often donate large amounts of money for university research, departments, clubs, and buildings. Last month, Joan Leung explained that Crest University's deal with Hyper Fuel earned her university extra money for research grants and funds for other programs. A university official said the money went to fellowships and research grants, as well as divvying up a share to the Students' Union and the Graduate Students' Association. Even if you never drink Hyper Fuel, you will benefit because our university can reap these rewards, so you will spend less money on tuition and other fees.

Exercise: Visualization

Continue your MMS outline in the Visualization Stage. First, ask yourself which style of visualization is best for your presentation: the positive, the negative, or the combined method?

Preferred method: ____

Now, make a list of benefits and/or risks that could exist in the future:

Finally, make a list of emotional words and images you can use in your speech:

Positive	Negative

Your audience will now be very eager to see your solution work and to have a better future. You can now ask for their physical help.

Step 5: Action

You need your audience members' help because solutions do not happen on their own. You must give your audience very specific actions to take right now. These actions will help implement and carry out your big solution. There are two parts to the Action Stage:

Give a review of your main points. You have made your audience aware of a problem, proposed a sensible solution, and made them realize what will happen in the future. Remind them of these things by restating your overview.

Call your audience to action. Think about the solution you proposed in the Satisfaction Stage. What can the members of the audience do to help the solution? Tell the audience members what to do. Act like a professor, and give your audience a real-world homework assignment. There are three rules you must follow when calling your audience to action.

I. **The action must be specific and detailed.**	You never want your audience to have to do more research. If they do not have all the necessary information, they will not do anything. Be sure to include names, addresses, email addresses, websites, dates, times, locations, and any other important information.
II. **The action must be easy and simple.**	People are usually busy, lazy, or both busy and lazy. Audience members will not follow difficult instructions. If the action is easy, many people will do it, and many people performing small tasks can lead to big results. Remember to think KISS : Keep It Simple Silly.
III. **The action must be immediate.**	The problem you described is happening right now, and the solution needs to happen as soon as possible. Therefore, your audience needs to take action immediately. Give them an action they can do now or on the same day, and give them a deadline, so they will not procrastinate.

Calling for Action

Your specific call to action will depend on your opinion. Does your opinion call for a change in audience members' lives? Presentations calling for changes in your audience members' lives will have easier action steps.

Example thesis calling for personal changes:

University students should see the new Wizard and Warlock movie.

Example actions:

First, you should go online and find the movie times and location. You can find that information on www.movie.com. Second, call your friends, and find a movie time that works for everyone.
Third, buy tickets either online or at the cinema. Finally, sit in the theater, and enjoy the movie.

These are simple steps that everyone knows about, but you must include them.

Does your thesis call for making non-personal changes in large institutions, such as universities, governments, businesses, or organizations? How can your audience create change in big institutions?

Some ideas of possible actions are talking to and persuading other people on the issue, persuading other people to take action, joining organizations, writing letters to officials, visiting officials in person, boycotting products or businesses, protesting, writing letters to the media, blogging, street advertising, contacting lawyers, joining lawsuits, spreading information to other people, and other activities. These actions are effective when a lot of people do them.

Problems to Avoid

Do not simply tell your audience to write a letter to the government. This action is considered vague and too weak. Below are some weak and strong examples of action:

Weak action: Write a letter to the government.
Strong action: Today, type a letter to the President of the United States. In the letter, include a strong statement about the issue. Make it clear to the President that we will not put up with this new policy. I have uploaded an example letter on my website, www.mysite.com/123. You are free to copy and paste my letter. Finally, put the letter in an envelope, and mail it to: The President of The United States of America, 1600 Pennsylvania Ave NW, Washington, DC 20500, USA. You can also call the White House at (202) 456-1111.

Weak action: Do not go to Dandy Donuts.
Strong action: From March 1st to March 31st, join the nationwide boycott of Dandy Donuts. First, sign the petition on the boycott website at www.stopdandydonuts.com. Next, do not enter or purchase anything from Dandy Donuts during the month of March. Later, when you pass by Dandy Donuts, hand out one of the "Stop Dandy Donuts" fliers to customers entering the store. I have a stack of fliers available for you today.

Example Action Stage: Today, you have heard why the current lack of Hyper Fuel at our university is unacceptable. You understand how the university can get Hyper Fuel on campus, and you have heard about the valuable benefits we would get. Students and faculty need to talk with, write letters to, and write emails to our university officials. Before Friday, please write to Dean Smith at 1200 Main Street, Anytown, NY, 52525. Demand Hyper Fuel in your letter. You can also call the dean at 555-1234. In addition to a letter and phone campaign, I am organizing a boycott of drinks purchased on campus. Please buy all your drinks off campus when possible, even soda and coffee. The short-term sacrifice of buying drinks off-campus will yield the future benefits of having Hyper Fuel and more funding on campus. Join the campaign for Hyper Fuel on campus not only for Kim Minsu's sake, but also for the sake and well-being of everyone at our wonderful university.

It may be helpful to give specific information to your audience on a visual aid or on a handout after your speech. It is hard to remember specific addresses and numbers, and many audience members may not be ready to write them down.

Exercise: Take Action!

It is time to complete your personal MMS outline with the Action Stage. First, write three specific things your audience members can do that are both easy and immediate. Then, write the specific details your audience needs to complete their assignment.

	Action 1	**Action 2**	**Action 3**
What should they do?			
When should they do it?			
Where should they go?			
Who should they talk to?			
How should they do it?			

MMS: The After Effects

MMS can produce immediate and lasting effects on the world around you. Days or weeks after your presentation, talk with audience members about their actions and update them on any progress that has occurred. You will not convince everyone to agree with you, and you will not convince everyone, who agrees with you, to take action. That is natural and expected; however, take pride in the people you do persuade, and feel empowered in the changes you make in the real world.

Structure Transcript

Good morning everyone. My name is Hyerim Jang. To get started, I would like to ask you a question. Which border between two countries is the most heavily militarized border in the world? You might think it is the border between Israel and the West Bank, but it is not. Actually, it is the Demilitarized Zone (DMZ) between North and South Korea. Today, I would like to tell you why South Korea is an important focal point in the world. By the end of this presentation, you will have a much better understanding of this vital yet often overlooked country. My talk will be divided into three parts: geographical location, economic strengths, and technological advances. Now, let's begin.

Korea has a very significant geographic position. Korea lies strategically at the center of Northeast Asia. This has meant Korea has long been considered very important by regional powers. Depending on how you look at it, Korea can be viewed as a gateway to Japan in the east and/or continental Asia in the west. Historically, Korea's location attracted the attention of bigger and more important powers like the Mongols, the Chinese, and the Japanese. This has resulted in a long and troublesome history. Today, South Korea is politically important because of its neighbor to the north. Every time North Korea starts saber rattling, the world looks to the South to see how best the North can be dealt with. Tied very closely to the South's political importance is military significance. The South's military alliance with the U.S. acts as a counterbalance to North Korea's aggression and China's untested military might. This uneasy alliance has come to define relations between these countries.

I have looked at the importance of Korea geographically. Now, let's look at the country's economic strengths. In financial and commercial terms, Korea is a shining example of an economy that has made the transformation from industrial minnow to post-industrial, service-based economic superpower. You only need to see the power of the KOSPI as a regional stock index to understand the importance of Korean finance. This can also be seen in foreign direct investment. In real terms, Korean institutions are the largest foreign investors in Vietnam and Cambodia, the second largest investors in Central Asia, and the third largest investors in China. All of this has helped to create a very large economy. This is remarkable given that at the cessation of fighting in 1953, the Republic of Korea was one of the poorest countries in the world and viewed as an international quagmire. Today, GDP exceeds US$20,000 per capita, and homegrown corporations like Samsung, LG, and Hyundai are synonymous with success.

I have discussed Korea's economic importance, but how do the country's technological advances make it a vital international hub? Today, Hyundai Motors is the sixth largest car manufacturer in the world. If Kia, a subsidiary of Hyundai, is included, then Hyundai Motors is on the cusp of ranking fourth in size and sales. Hyundai's success can be attributed to two key factors: engine research and development and creating cheaper more efficient manufacturing processes. Combined, Hyundai was able to recast itself as a leader in automotive production, design, and reliability. Hyundai is also the world's number one manufacturer of ships. Again, they have been able to redefine the manufacturing process. Hyundai was quick to understand that no two ships are the same. Each ship producer needs to meet the exact requirements of the owners. By creating a modular ship-building system, Hyundai has been able to mass produce many parts while meeting their clients' specific needs and wants. This has led to cheaper high quality ships. Finally, Korea is probably most famous for electronics. At the heart of this success is the semiconductor industry. Korea is home to two of the largest semi-conductor companies in the world, Hynix and Samsung. Through extensive research and development, these companies have revolutionized electronics. You cannot always see the Korean influence in a product, but the next time you open your Sony VAIO or Apple Mac Book, know the chips powering those machines are from Samsung. This has helped catapult Samsung to become the number one electronics company in the world.

I have reached the end of my presentation regarding South Korea's important role in the world. First, I discussed Korea's geographical importance. Remember that it is located between large, industrialized, political and economic powerhouses. Second, I examined the strength of South Korea's economy. Do not forget that Korea plays a key role in Asian financial markets. Finally, I looked at examples of South Korea's cutting edge technology. Please keep in mind that this small country is at the forefront of the semi-conductor and LCD industries. As you can see, for such a small country, Korea plays a crucial role internationally. Not too long ago, the Korean Peninsula was left devastated by the Korean War. Since then, South Korea has transformed itself from a poor third world country to a vibrant star amongst the developed world. This is a feat most countries cannot claim, so the next time someone says, "Korea? Where's that?" Just say, "It's a shining example of Asia." Thank you. Now, if you have any questions, I would like to take time to answer them.

Informative Presentation Transcript

Good morning everybody. My name is Han Ji-hye, and it is my pleasure to be standing before you all today. I love living in Korea! Korea is a great country with everything I need to live a happy, long, and secure life. I can't imagine living anywhere else. However, I know that there are those of you who one day dream of going abroad, settling down, and living the good live. This raises the question, what is the best country in the world to live in? Of course, this differs from person to person. For example, if you don't like mountains and sheep, New Zealand would be a bad choice. Anyway, every year internationalliving.com surveys the countries of the world and ranks them from highest to lowest. Surprisingly, Korea was not number 1. We came in 42nd place. Today, we will look at the top three countries and discover what makes these countries great places to live.

According to internationalliving.com, the third best country in the world to live in is Switzerland. For precision in every field, there is no country that can beat Switzerland. If you take a Swiss train, you know it will arrive on time. If you see a Swiss doctor, you know you will get the right diagnosis. If you take Swiss medicine, you know you are not swallowing poison. Switzerland ranks as one of the most expensive places in the world to live, but this is offset by a stunningly clean and beautiful environment, a strong and vibrant economy, and a very cosmopolitan population. Switzerland is truly a land where everything works.

Second on the list was the "Lucky Country", Australia. One of the reasons Australia scored well was its relatively strong economy. Because Australia is a mineral-rich country, Australia has prospered through the sale of iron, gold, and silver to resource hungry emerging Asian countries like China, India, and Vietnam. The boom economy has also led to generous spending by the Australian government in the areas of infrastructure and healthcare, making it one of the best English-speaking countries in these two areas. However, what makes Australia truly special is the Aussie way of life. Australians place a premium on having fun. This is why the beach is so special for Australians, not to mention the great Australian barbecue and cold beer. Australians work hard, but they play even harder. All these things combine to make Australia a great place to live.

The best country to live in on the list also happens to be the most visited country in the world. That's right, in first place is France. France, the jewel in the crown of Europe. Despite the fact many French complain about the massive bureaucracy and high taxes, France offers her citizens the very best in healthcare, education, and welfare. What makes France even more appealing is there is something for everyone. For fashionistas, there are the trendy Parisian boulevards, crammped with contemporary and vintage men's and women's styles. On the other hand, the countryside abounds with some of the world's best vegetables, fruits, meat, and great wines. In fact, all of France is a gourmet's paradise. To the south are the beautiful towns, cities, and beaches of the Riviera, and to the south-west are world-class surf beaches. For art and history buffs, the options are limitless. Above all, the French know how to take advantage of what France has to offer, and they know how to live well, and this more than anything else makes France the best country to live in.

There is no doubt the three countries covered today are all great places to live. Switzerland is not a bad place to be if you value timeliness. Australia is a great choice for those who value quality beer and quality downtime. France is a great place for those who love life - especially the good things in life. So, if you are thinking of moving abroad, these are three great options. However, remember wherever you come from, there really is no place that compares to home. I hope you are happy wherever you may end up. Thank you.

Demonstrative Presentation Transcript

I bet you all 5000 won that if I went to your homes, I could find one thing in the kitchen cupboard. Do you know what that item is? Yes, ladies and gentlemen, it is *ramen*. Ramen has long been a big part of the Korean diet. It is a quick, low-fuss meal that takes only minutes to prepare. But, what makes *ramen* special is we all have our styles and preferences when it comes to preparing this great dish. My name is Jung Sangbae, and today I'm going to show you how to make "Sangbae's Special Ramen."

Before you get started with the actual cooking, you need to go to your local supermarket and buy some ingredients. For normal *ramen*, I suggest you go to the noodle aisle and make your selection. My personal favorite is *Shin Ramen* from the good people at the Nong Shim Corporation. For

"Sangbae's Special Ramen," you will need *ramen*, eggs, *kimchi*, *mandu* (Korean dumplings), *ddeok* (a type of Korean rice cake), spring onions, onions, and minced garlic.

After you arrive home, cut the onions into fine rings, slice the spring onions into two to three centimeter lengths, and fill a pot with about 500 milliliters to a liter of water. Then, put the pot on the stove, and once the water has started to boil, add the noodles. Boil the noodles for about three minutes.

Now, this is where it gets interesting! Inside the *ramen* packet, you will find the flavoring and seasoning. Next, open the packet, and pour the contents into the boiling water and noodle concoction. Once you have done this, you have the run-of-the-mill, standard *ramen*. However, for the true noodle connoisseur, this is not enough. I will now put a healthier twist on this very common meal.

The first thing you should do is add the onion and garlic to the mix. The onion needs to be added early to make it soft. Then add the *ddeok* and sliced spring onion. Don't add the *ddeok* too late, or it will be too chewy. About a minute later, it is time to add the *mandu*. If the *mandu* is frozen, you should add it earlier. Finally, it is time to add the egg. Break the egg into the small bowl, and beat it with a whisk. Then, pour the egg into the soup.

To finish off, get a deep bowl, and pour the *ramen* into the bowl. Mmmmmmm, that smells delicious. All that is left is to eat and enjoy it!

There are many different types of *ramen* on the market and infinite ways of preparing this iconic dish. Today, I have shown you what works for me. The next time you have an urge for *ramen*, why not try this style? Your stomach and taste buds will thank you! Bon appétit!

Persuasive Presentation Transcript

Good afternoon ladies and gentlemen; my name is Ahn Junyeong.

"Wake up!" "Now, wait!" "Walk!" "Smoke them if you have them!" "Run!" "Stop!" "Sleep!" "Eat!" "Say, 'Goodbye girlfriend!'" Gentlemen, get ready to hear these words shouted at you every day for two years of your life. Warfare has been around for as long as humankind has been wandering the Earth. Throughout history, society has always been organized to deal with the threat of attack culminating in the national armies of today. Modern military forces can be divided into two types: professional volunteer forces and part or full conscript forces. In Korea, we have a part conscription force, meaning it is a mix of conscript and professional soldiers. Many people argue conscription is the duty of all Korean men. They argue we must protect our motherland at all costs. However, Korean conscription is grossly unfair because it wastes government money, steals time away from young men, and does not offer fair compensation.

To begin with, maintaining a conscript army costs the Korean taxpayer a huge amount every year. According to the Korean Ministry of Defense, conscription and maintaining a conscript army, accounted for 58 percent of Korea's defense budget in 2009. To put that in dollar terms, the real cost of Korea's conscript army was US$7.8 billion. This is more than the GDP of New Zealand and Ireland combined and accounts for more than state spending in health and education respectively. According to Lee Hyeonhun, the Opposition Minister for Defense, this is an unfair burden for the citizens of Korea. "Every year the cost of living goes up, and our taxes rise, too. This is too much for average people. One way to bring down taxes is do away with conscription," Mr. Lee said. Also, according to the Association of Concerned Korean Citizens, as defense spending goes up, government spending on infrastructure and welfare has been falling in real terms. The website for the Association of Concerned Korean Citizens stated, "The expense of providing a better future for all Koreans, young and old, has now been passed into the hands of the individual because our government is obsessed with creating and maintaining a vast and pointless military force."

Not only is a conscript force expensive, but it also wastes the time of conscripted soldiers. All men have to give up two years of their lives which could be spent doing better things. This puts Korean men at a distinct disadvantage compared to their peers in other countries. For example, according to a leading recruitment company, GGYM, to qualify for an upper management track position with the World Bank or the IMF, you need to join the workforce before the age of 30 and have three years post-doctoral experience in a related NGO or academic institution. The two years Korean men spend in the military means it is almost impossible for them to gain access to these organizations, leaving Korean men under-represented. In Singapore, which also has compulsory military service, soldiers have the option to learn practical skills they can take into the real world. According to David Chang, the Singaporean Minister of Labor, 25 years ago the Singaporean government came to the realization that conscripted soldiers were wasting their time locked away in barracks. He said the government decided it was best to offer them courses like accounting, finance, automotive repair, and engineering. These are all useful outside the confines of the military.

Finally, to add to the cost and time issues, conscription is wrong because conscripts are inadequately compensated for their time. The average conscript is given an allowance of KRW80,000 per month. This is peanuts. Israel has a policy of compulsory military for both men and women. According to the Israeli Ministry of Statistics, the average male soldier receives of a one off payment of US$30,000 when he is discharged from military service, more if he saw active service. This is paid on top of a regular salary. Former Israeli soldiers are also eligible for free tuition through Israeli state owned universities. A similar system exists in Switzerland and Germany. In both countries, conscripts are paid a wage that exceeds the minimum wage, and they are given university credit relative to the time they spend in service. In addition to this, in both Switzerland and Germany, conscripts can opt for a variety of types of service, as long as they can prove what they are doing is in the national interest. The big thing here is, again, the conscripted can draw wages or a salary based on market rates.

It is clear that compulsory military service is wrong at every level. Specifically, taxpayers' money spent on the military is wasted and would be better spent elsewhere. It also uses up young Korean men's time when they are in the prime of their lives, and it leaves them unable to tackle other opportunities. On top of this, Korean men are tremendously under-compensated for their sacrifice. Some argue military service is a form of modern slavery. While this is clearly an exaggeration, we need to give more back to the brave young men who give so much and receive so little in the name of keeping our nation secure. Better yet, we could do away with it altogether. Thank you.

Seminar Group Presentation Transcript: Body Image

When you look in the mirror, are you satisfied with what you see? Are there things about your physical appearance you want to change? If you have answered 'yes' ladies and gentlemen, you are not alone. Have you ever asked yourself why you are unhappy with your body? Why, as humans, do we strive to fit a very specific body shape? Having a standard of beauty is important. It is a measure of how we view and evaluate those around us. In recent years, we have seen the phenomenon of 'lookism' and all its modern manifestations. Good morning everybody. Today my team members and I are going to teach you about body image. First, we will give some history on body image. Next, we will talk about how once the standard of beauty was a cultural construct that differs from place to place, culture to culture, but today is becoming homogenized. Finally, we will look at the standard of beauty in Korea, and how it is enforced by the media.

The history of body image is as varied and interesting as history itself. Throughout the ages, we have defined and redefined what it means to be beautiful or handsome. However, the idea of being attractive goes beyond this. Leading anthropologist and zoologist, Prof. Martin Styles, agues attraction is a biological imperative. As in the animal kingdom, humans need to be attracted to those of the opposite sex to maintain a population. If we fast forward a few hundred thousand years past hunter-gathers and into civilization, we see an interesting phenomenon. Unlike most of the animal kingdom, human females are the focus of attraction. One place we can see this is in western art. During the Renaissance period the standard of beauty in art was clear. Fuller figured women were viewed as attractive. The standard for men was unclear, but if Davinci and Michelangelo were anything to go by, the ideal male form was fit and muscular. At the same time in Korea, we can see from the art of the Joseon period that the ideal woman was small and demure, with a large round face, and small eyes, lips, feet, and hands. If we fast forward to the twentieth century with its innovations in mass media technologies, we start to see rapid changes in standards of beauty across the world.

Traditionally, standards of beauty have been largely based on cultural factors. In certain cultures, being fat was considered a plus because it meant one had the means and resources for survival. In other cultures, having muscle mass for both men and women was viewed as desirable because it symbolized hard work. Today, however, things seem to be changing. With the advent of American driven globalization, we can see a more uniform standard of beauty emerge in many countries. What I am referring to is a standard of beauty that is largely sexual and based almost entirely on physical attributes. This change has caused a lot controversy in India. Indian films, affectionately referred to as Bollywood films, lead Indian popular culture. Over the past decade, women in these films have been exposing more and more flesh while using their bodies to create a more overtly sexual message. Many elements within Indian society have blamed foreign influences for this and have demanded the Indian government to take action. Traditionally, the female form was not widely seen in Indian films. Indian academics have linked an increase in eating disorders among young Indian women to the portrayal of the female form in film and are also calling for tighter restrictions. In Nigeria, where a fuller figured man and woman have been the accepted standard of beauty, things are changing, too. Even in the most remote parts of the country, it is possible to get low cost or free satellite television. As a result, people on the fringes of global society have been able to access a plethora of new information from all over the world. Leading Nigerian journalist Levi Obojobifor said this has changed the way Nigerians see the world and themselves. He said, there has been a surge in consumerism, and, more interestingly, many Nigerian women have started to diet in an effort to change their body shapes. He said, television shows like *America's Next Top Model* tell women they can lead exciting lives if they conform to a certain body shape. He also added this is often portrayed as a way out of poverty. What is the situation in Korea? Let's welcome our next speaker.

Korea has one of the narrowest standards of beauty. This may have something to do with the homogenous nature of Korean society, but leading academics in the field are divided on the issue. The fact remains, what we view as beautiful or handsome lays within very narrow boundaries. 'S-line bodies' and 'V-shaped faces' are terms you can hear everywhere. If you do not believe us, why, on a percentage basis, do more Korean men and women undergo potentially life threatening surgical procedures than any other national group in the hopes of becoming more attractive? Why are such huge numbers of our young men and women starving themselves? Last year the nutritionists from the International Council of Universities conducted a study on female university students from 102 countries. They were primarily concerned with looking at diet and eating patterns. They discovered more than 80 percent of Korean female university students were underweight, and more than 70 percent were engaged in some form of dieting. In both categories, Korea was number one. The thinnest women are dieting the most. We surveyed 300 female students to find out more. We found that almost all of them were dissatisfied with their appearance and were engaged in some form of activity to change their outward appearance. Why is this happening? According to media expert Prof. Kang Minji, the way we understand the world around us is through the messages we receive from the media. If we are constantly bombarded with a certain message, that message becomes part of our sub-conscious, and this is true in the case of body image. There is no escaping it. Everywhere we look, we see images of what ideal men and women should look like.

Conceptions of body image are a hugely important part of our identities. This is nothing new. The way a person looks gives us important clues on what kind of person we are dealing with including ideas about their background, social status, and character. However, when body image becomes an unrealistic and potentially life threatening burden to people, we should stop and ask ourselves, "Is it really so important?" In Korea and around the world, we need to accept that people come in many different shapes and sizes and move beyond such a narrow standard of beauty. Thank you.

Seminar Group Presentation Transcript: The Death Penalty

Crime and Punishment. When you hear these words you may think of a really long stuffy book written by a nineteenth century Russian author. This may be true. However, the debate surrounding actual crimes and appropriate punishments is alive and well. At the core of this debate is the argument over the death penalty. Debate over the imposition and use of the death penalty is as old as crime, and the topic has been polarizing opinions for just as long. Some say the death penalty is a brutal and barbaric practice that flies in the face of civilized society. Others maintain the punishment needs to fit the crime. Today, we will examine the death penalty in detail. Let's begin with our first presenter.

The death penalty is a reasonable punishment for heinous crimes because it can be cost effective. The cost of incarcerating a prisoner for life is huge. According to the British Ministry of Justice, last year the average cost of keeping someone locked up was about GBP41,000. In America, for the same period, the cost of keeping a prisoner under lock and key was about US$35,000. In Korea, the same cost was around KRW30 million per year. Opponents of the death penalty argue that the cost of putting someone to death is more than keeping them in prison for life. As it stands, this is true. However, this accepts there is really no way to shave costs off putting someone to death. By circumventing the very costly appeals process, lowering the standard of care for death row inmates, and coming up with cheaper and more efficient methods of execution, we can save the taxpayer hundreds of millions of won. For example, in the American state of Texas, the main method of execution is lethal injection. Now, to kill a person in this manor costs somewhere in the region of US$300,000. Why waste all that money when a bullet or a length of rope costs less than a dollar?

Thanks for that. The death penalty is justifiable not only because of its cost effectiveness, but also because it is final. There is no chance the guilty will be able to commit the offense again. We live in a scientific age. We have the benefit of DNA testing which has drastically cut the instances of wrongful convictions. With this increased certainty, we can be confident those, who commit the most dreadful crimes against individuals and society, will never have the opportunity to be repeat offenders. Modern history is littered with instances of killers serving a sentence and being set free, only to go on to commit the same crime again. One such example was Texan Katy Davis who observed three strangers outside her Austin apartment. Did she confront them? No, she turned and walked away. Later, when she returned, she was attacked by paroled convicted murderer Charles Rector and two other male accomplices. The men ransacked her apartment, abducted her and took her to a lake where she was beaten, gang-raped, shot in the head, and repeatedly forced underwater until she drowned. If Charles Rector had been given the death sentence, Katy Davis would still be alive today. How do you think her family feels?

Thank you both. You give some compelling reasons why we should support the death penalty. However, the reasons against the death penalty outweigh those in favor of it. First, we, as a society, have to move away from the "eye for an eye" revenge mentality if civilization is to advance. The "eye for an eye" mentality will never solve anything. A revenge philosophy inevitably leads to an endless cycle of violence. At some point, we need to really think deeply about what separates us from animals and apply that humanity to society. What kind of society can condemn murder, but at the same time allow the state to kill in the name of justice? Doesn't this seem hypocritical? Many death penalty advocates argue the death penalty acts as a deterrent. If this is so, why in the People's Republic of China, which is the largest proponent of the death penalty in the world, has the incidence of violent crime and the imposition of the death penalty both seen an exponential increase in the last few years? The same is true in Texas. I'll now pass the floor over to the next presenter.

Thanks. You make some excellent points. At this time, I'd like to ask a question. Do you think the application of the death penalty provides closure for the victims' families? In some cases, maybe the answer is 'yes'. However, in many cases the answer in 'no'. Imagine having someone else's blood on your hands. Is killing another person going to bring a loved one back to life? Most definitely not. It defies logic. Matters are made even worse if the wrong person is convicted of the crime. Despite improvements in forensic science, there are still many mistakes made. Last year in Florida, Henry Jackson was found guilty of the slaying of Paul Connor. Jackson was found guilty on the strength of DNA evidence. It was later found that Jackson was not guilty, and the jury in the case had relied too much on the DNA evidence, while ignoring other, more compelling evidence. This is becoming so common that leading academics have dubbed it the "CSI Effect".

There is no doubt the death penalty is a thorny topic. There are merits and demerits to both sides of the argument. In recent decades, Korean society has undergone a wondrous transformation, and there is little doubt many aspects of living in Korea have improved. However, with the good comes the bad. The rise in consumerism, changes in family, and the population drift toward urban areas have all contributed to an exponential rise in violent crime at every level of Korean society. If we, as a society, decide to keep and employ the death penalty in capital convictions, we need to look to the examples of places like Texas and Florida, and to some extent China, to learn from their successes and failures. Thank you.

Body Language Transcript

How many times have you tried to lose weight, but been unsuccessful? Today, I'm going to let you in on a little secret and tell you how you can shed unwanted pounds. By the end of this presentation, you will know how easy it is to have the body you have always wanted. My talk is divided into three parts. First, eat food you love. Second, your stomach can't fool you: you can fool your stomach. Third, sleep yourself to a thinner, happier you. Now, let's get started.

Voice Transcript

Good afternoon ladies and gentlemen, my name is Ahn Seulgi, and I'm a representative for PEN (Protect the Environment Now). Yellow dust in the air that we breathe, acid rain that makes our hair fall out, heavy metals in water that are found in the fish we eat. All of these are examples of how pollution directly affects each of us. Today, I'd like to examine the socio-economic effects of pollution, and this presentation will shed light on the gravity of the planet's current situation and underline the need for change. First, I'll look at pollution in relation to food output. Next, I'll discuss how pollution hinders development. Finally, I'll suggest some steps we can take to solve these problems.

Eye Contact Transcript

The word euthanasia comes from two Greek words *eu* (which means *good*) and *thanatos* (which means *death*). As you guessed, this word literally means mercy killing. Now, I would like to discuss euthanasia, and while there is much controversy surrounding this topic, my intention is not to choose sides but instead to present both viewpoints, so we can have a more complete understanding of the issues underlying this debate. Therefore, I will first look at the merits in support of it, and then move on to examine the demerits in opposition of it.

Visual Aid Transcript

What do Bae Yongjun, Rain, and Yun Eunhye all have in common? That's right! They are all international Korean entertainers, and they play an important role in *hallyu*. For those of you who do not know *hallyu*, it is the spread of Korean culture throughout the world through various media outlets such as television, movies, and music. Today, I'd like to examine the effects of *hallyu* on other countries in Southeast Asia to see whether or not the impact has been positive or negative. First, I'll look at Vietnam, then I'll move on to Malaysia, and I'll finally finish off with Thailand.

Question and Answer Script

Example 1 - Poor Question
Presenter: Thank you for listening to my presentation. Please raise your hand if you have a question.

Audience member: Thanks for the presentation on the declining birthrate in most OECD countries. I learned a lot. My question is about your shoes. They are really cool. Where did you get them?

Presenter: I'm sorry, but can you limit your questions to the contents of my presentation. We can talk about what I'm wearing later.

Example 2 - Poor Answer
Presenter: Thank you for listening to my presentation. Please raise your hand if you have a

question.

Audience member: Thanks for your presentation on the declining birthrate in most OECD countries. You covered the problems associated with this phenomenon. Can you offer a solution please?

Presenter: Errrr, I think the declining birthrate is a big issue. I told you why. Next question.

Example 3 - Model Question and Answer

Presenter: Thank you for listening to my presentation. Please raise your hand if you have a question.

Audience member: Thanks for your presentation on the declining birthrate in most OECD countries. You covered the problems associated with this phenomenon. Can you offer a solution please?

Presenter: Well... thank you for your question. Your question is about finding a solution to the declining birthrate. I think the best way to increase the birthrate is through government support for working parents. This could come in the form of a tax break, or it could take the form of greater government financial assistance with childcare. If the government could shoulder some of the financial burden of raising children, that would go a long way to ensure there will be more children in the future. Does that answer your question?

Audience member: Yes, thank you.

Monroe's Motivated Speech Transcript

In George Orwell's famous novel, *1984*, citizens are monitored by the government 24 hours a day. They are watched, they are listened to, and they are told what they can and cannot say. If a citizen is found guilty of improper speech, especially against the government, the person is taken away by the government. Though *1984* was a novel published in 1949, the idea of the government monitoring citizens for anti-government thoughts still exists today. We sometimes think of countries like Iran, Turkmenistan, and North Korea, but these actions also occur here in South Korea. The real-name Internet system was established in 2005, and since then, the government has been able to monitor and record the opinions of Internet users on South Korean websites. Today, I'm going to tell you why the South Korean government should get rid of the real-name Internet system. I'll tell you about the problems we face with the real-name system, the Internet policy we should have, and the benefits the new policy will have.

There are many problems with the real-name Internet system. First of all, South Korea is the only country in the world that has this kind of system. Sure, it is better than being banned from speaking freely on the Internet like in China, but it is much more restrictive than other democratic countries.

Second of all, citizens must register their names with Korean websites, but not with foreign websites. Anyone wanting to speak freely on the Internet can do so easily. We saw this happen in 2009 when YouTube and Google did not comply with the South Korean government and refused to make people register their real names with their websites. South Korean websites may be losing business to foreign websites because of the real-name system. People may feel safer by joining foreign websites that do not require their true identity. Finally, having the real-name Internet system gives the government too much power. Even if people trust the government right now, we may not be able to trust the government in the future. Many German people trusted Adolf Hitler at first, but then later learned he could not be trusted at all. Our conversations and ideas are recorded right now, and this leaves us vulnerable to our ideas being used against us by the government. In order to stop these crimes against the Korean people, the laws need to change.

The real-name Internet system should be abolished in the Republic of Korea. The president or the National Assembly needs to immediately make a new law that says no citizen must use their real name or ID on South Korean websites. They should state that they respect individuals' privacy and free speech. Next, Korean websites should erase all citizens' names and ID numbers from records and anything they posted. After that, Korean citizens and anyone on Korean websites should speak their mind freely like people do in other democratic countries in order to promote discussion. There are many good things that will happen in the future if we get rid of the real-name Internet system.

If we don't have the real-name Internet system, people will speak freely on the Internet about all issues. For one thing, even if someone speaks about something unpopular, they won't have to fear being punished for their personal opinion. Free discussion is the best way to reach the truth and to solve problems. Yes, we will have to read opinions we don't like, but we are civilized enough to do that. A second benefit is that the government will never be able to use our ideas against us. If the Korean government ever changes for the worse, like Hitler's Germany changed, we won't have to live in fear of it hunting us down for our beliefs. Also, if South Korea is ever taken over by another country, we won't have to worry about the oppressors using our posts on the Internet against us, our families and our friends. Finally, if we don't have the real-name Internet system, we can create more business with Koreans and foreigners because they won't have to be afraid to use their real names.

Today, I have reviewed the problems with the real-name Internet system. I told you about my solution of getting rid of the real-name system, and I shared the benefits of having more freedom on the Internet. We can't make these changes for the good without each other, though. Today, I need you to log on and join the website www.nomorerealname.com. It is hosted in the USA and doesn't require your real name. There, you will find the email addresses of the president and other people in the government. Write them emails this week and ask them to change the real-name Internet system. Be sure to include the sentence "Get rid of the real-name Internet law." Finally, get your friends and family to visit the website and write emails. One day, we can live in a nation with freer Internet laws like other democratic countries in the world.

Here is a list of websites that can provide you with creative ideas, help you add more value to your presentation, and show you what to do and what not to do during a presentation.

www.animoto.com

This is an interesting site that allows you to upload you pictures and text to its server, and then its software will automatically create a very stunning movie clip which includes your pictures, text, and even music. This definitely has plenty of **_WOW factor_** and would make a good opener for a presentation. The website is user friendly, and it offers free trial versions of its software. It is also possible to get the upgraded version for free as long as it is used for educational purposes.

www.corbis.com

Ever wonder where to find amazingly stunning pictures that are high resolution and can be used freely? If you have, then this is the website for you. This site has tons of breathtaking and creative pictures. Literally, it has a picture for anything and everything you can think of. When you become a member (which is free), you can download and save wonderful photos and images free of watermarks. Although you will want to read the legal disclaimer, you may use the photos freely as long as it is for educational purposes, and you do not profit from the use of the photos. You have been warned!

www.dafont.com

Are you tired of the same old fonts that come standard with MS Office? Need something unique, extravagant, or creative? Look no further. This website has it all. There are hundreds of free fonts that are easy to download and use. These eye-catching fonts are guaranteed to impress your audience while adding that little extra finesse to personalize your PowerPoint and make it truly something different.

www.images.google.com

Although this seems like a no-brainer, Google Images is a wonderful source of photos. You can find a plethora of pictures, cartoons, charts, graphs, and diagrams. You name it, and it is there. The only downfall is that you have to be careful about the quality of the images. There are many low-resolution pictures that simply will not be satisfactory as visual aids.

www.pecha-kucha.org

20 images in 20 seconds. This is the main guideline behind the Pecha Kucha format. This method allows for the presentation to focus on brevity and conciseness. While this format may not be suitable for you, this website provides many real presentations and PowerPoint slides created by designers from around the world. This site is definitely worth looking into, especially to get ideas for your own visual aids.

www.presentationzen.com

This website focuses on the visual component or message of your presentation. There are many good ideas and examples, plus there are links to other useful sites. If you are concerned about the design and layout of your visual aids, then check out this website.

www.prezi.com

This website proves that there is more than just PowerPoint when it comes to visual aids. The software on the site allows you to create interesting visuals that you create on a canvas. It is difficult to put into words, so you should check out the demo video online. The software is extremely user-friendly and easy to learn. The trial version is free, but if you want upgrades, you will need to pay annual fees. In addition, this site makes use of cloud computing, so your work is automatically saved and backed-up on its server, and you can access it anywhere and at anytime.

www.slideshare.net

This website allows you to upload your own PowerPoint presentations to its website, so you can share your ideas with people all over the world. What is great about this site is that you can browse through thousands of PowerPoint presentations, and again, many of them are great and many are horrible, but by spending some time perusing them, you can easily see what works well and what does not when it comes to making your own PowerPoints.

www.ted.com

This website contains many interesting and insightful presentations given by some of the world's most important and influential scholars, politicians, and businesspeople. What is good about this site is that it is free, and you can see many examples of both good and bad presentations. It is a wonderful reminder that just because you are an expert in your field, that does not make you a professional presenter!